SOARING

7 LESSONS TO HELP YOU SOAR INTO THE LIFE YOU WERE MEANT TO LIVE

MADE 2 SOAR

Made 2 Soar
P.O. Box 83
Jamestown, NC 27282
twitter.com/madetwosoar
www.made2soar.com

First published in the United States of America February 2017

ISBN-13: 978-0692832325

Mama didn't raise no fool!

This book is dedicated to the woman who gave me the DNA, words of wisdom, and Godly inspiration to live a life of distinction and purpose. Bearing witness to her life's transformation, courage, and perseverance has been a light of hope on my journey.
Thanks, Mom.

Acknowledgments

I am thankful for the wonderful team of gifted professionals who've made a difference in my life, and the lives of so many. To my book project team: James Murray and Laura A. (editors), Nader Aboulhosn and Melissa Ramgeet (videographers), Porlan Cunningham (public relations), and Jim Publicover (advisor) thank you for believing in me. Your expertise has helped me create, develop, and produce this book, which will reach and change countless lives.

To my church and spiritual home, Love & Faith Christian Fellowship, I give thanks. I've grown more solid in my understanding of my calling with every sermon given while I sat in the pews. I'm also grateful for the warm encouragement and conversations I've had on the campus grounds.

Pastor Thomas, thank you for being a clear example of God's grace, mercy, love, and favor. Because of your dedication to God, your messages have helped keep this former college student and current adult out of trouble. For I know that somewhere in the future, I look a whole lot better than I do right now!

To my family: All the love, encouragement, support, personal care, guidance, and embraces you've given me are all reasons why I have the guts to unapologetically be me. No words can adequately describe my gratitude for my dad (Augustus), mom (Angela), oldest sister (Tanya), brother-in-law (Aaron), nephews (Aaron, Ayden and Azael) and niece (Janyia), younger sisters (Melissa, Jennifer and Melanie) and aunt (Boniswa). I can only hope that the products of my labor pay off for each of you.

Finally, with everything that is in me, I give all of my praise and thanks to God. I am eternally grateful for His unfailing love for me. The reality is that without Him, I am nothing.

Table of Contents

Introduction

"So what will M2S stand for?" my sister asked as we sat staring at our blank sheets of paper. We were at our weekly brainstorming session, and I seemed to have left my brain elsewhere. I was without words, which made me a bit nervous. The unusual silence was beginning to feel uneasy, and no matter how much I tried to think positively, the unsettling question of What have I done? wouldn't leave my mind. The premature establishment of my brand proved to be one of my first screw-ups I made as a budding entrepreneur.

The need to rectify my error was a heavy weight on my shoulders, quite a different feeling from the optimism I entered the meeting with. I'd rolled in with a touch of arrogance, confident that the meeting would be a piece of cake. Surely I was capable of using my creativity and shifting the brand to capture a new concept, one that would adequately describe the grand endeavor I was ready to embark upon.

My drive to produce and my slightly presumptuous attitude overshadowed my ability to think clearly and ultimately stopped me in my tracks.

"What will M2S stand for?" asked my sister again, not certain if I'd heard her the first time. Her repetition almost sent me over the edge. My reaction had less to do with her questioning, and everything to do with disappointment in myself. Earning a marketing degree from my alma mater educated me on how important having the right brand is to the success of a company.

I became anxious, longing for the overflow of ideas and creativity that I was used to. But this time I had nothing. With only two of us at the table, I'm sure Melissa felt the frustration rising in me as I impatiently tapped the side of the table. Jaw clenched and lips pinched together, I shifted my weight and leaned back with a desperate sigh. The temptation to grow furious raised its ugly head and I struggled to subdue it. I was on the verge of calling it quits for the day. Meanwhile, Melissa sat across the table, as relaxed and cool as a cucumber.

"What about the word soar," she said nonchalantly. "Soar starts with *s*, what about Made 2 Soar?"

My eyes widening with surprise and elation, I exclaimed, "That's it! That's what we will call the business, Made 2 Soar!"

It's amazing how much a great idea can oil a squeaky wheel on an entrepreneurial train. In that moment, my enthusiasm skyrocketed. My attitude shifted from a sour state to that of gratitude. I was amazed by her. In all of her serenity, she allowed herself to be the vessel from which a God-idea flowed. Her suggestion was inspired divinely because it adequately encompassed the mindset I hoped to inspire others to adopt.

From that moment, Made 2 Soar was more than a title; it was a frame of mind and a movement. A movement that I was dedicated and passionate about pursuing.

By the time we returned home, my sheet of paper was no longer blanketed in white. I had written down Made 2 Soar at least three times and repeated it to myself at least a dozen. It flowed so well that I wanted to scream it from the mountaintop. Of course, I couldn't get up a mountain, so I figured sharing it on social media was just as meaningful.

Branding my business was just the beginning of something great. And because it meant so much to me, I wanted it to mean just as much to others. I wanted people to feel the electrifying empowerment that I'd felt at the mere mention of Made 2 Soar. In order for this to occur, I knew people had to be informed. They needed to know what it really meant to soar. What did soaring feel like? How do you even get off the ground?

If I wanted people to adopt soaring as a practice and a way of life, I had to understand it myself. The first word soaring brought to mind was success. Although such a definition was a bit clichéd, there was truth to the statement. Soaring is the act of succeeding.

While many people know this, there's still a dangerous number of us stuck on the ground. So many people are wandering aimlessly through life, unable to catch wind and fly to their highest potential. Why? The answer is simple. We limit success to certain areas of our lives. To some, success means having financial abundance. To others, success in its entirety only pertains to their family's quality of life. But I know succeeding isn't limited to enjoying one aspect of life. Success is the act of soaring—experiencing increase above the norm in all areas of life.

$$\bullet \bullet \bullet$$

I am grateful to have had the opportunity to speak to many audiences. Because of my unique life experiences, I'm called to present on a variety of exciting topics. I totally enjoy being onstage, for during that brief period, I have the undivided attention of the audience. Obviously, standing approximately two feet tall and riding around in a motorized wheelchair is what initially grabs everyone's attention. But onstage, I completely embrace that attention. Those moments become my opportunity to pour myself into the lives of those who will listen.

But can I let you in on a little secret (no pun intended)? There's something I love doing even more than being in the spotlight. I absolutely love impacting others in an unscripted manner. The unpredictability, personalization, and attention I'm able to offer during those moments create a special level of understanding, relatability, and growth for not only the individual I'm talking to, but for me, as well.

So it excites me when I'm graced with the opportunity to engage in Q&A sessions after my presentations. And even when this opportunity isn't afforded to me during an event, I make it my mission to interact with everyone gracious enough to listen. Why do I do this? Because the ability to go to the next level in life is contingent on a willingness to help, care for, and be genuine with those who might need an extra push.

Still, I wondered if there was something more I could do. There had to be a way to reach people I might never get a chance to meet. There had to be a way I could reach places I might never have the chance to visit. So I took a leap of faith and began to write *"SOARING!"*

Now you know my *why*, let me share with you the *what*. As you'll learn, one of my main reflections in this book is that while people are amazed by my physical appearance, as well as the challenges I've overcome and the success I've had in my life thus far, my personal astonishment at my growth on this journey is even more profound. However, the lessons I've learned and wisdom I've acquired mean very little unless I allow them to work in my life. One of the responsibilities of soaring is sharing your success with others.

In this book, my first piece of literature ever, I hope to share with you the principles of success that are essential to our ability to grow and soar.

LESSON ONE

Discover, Proclaim, and Implement Your Why

"

SUCCESS WITHOUT A STORY OR A PURPOSE IS HOLLOW AND UNFULFILLING.

"

@madetwosoar

I'll never forget the piercing disappointment in my heart as I rolled out of my final afternoon IEP meeting. I was finally in my senior year of high school, eager to break free from hallways lined with lockers and teenage gossip that, as the days went by, increasingly lost its appeal. Most of my peers were deeply invested in after-school clubs, enjoying the freedom of having their own cars and, of course, planning for prom. Prom is a huge event for most seniors. Besides graduation, it's the last chance for many kids to experience an unforgettable night of fun with their high school friends.

Call me an odd kid, but my focus was elsewhere. I spent more of my time making sure my senior projects were completed, applying for scholarships, and receiving college admissions. These events were the highlights of my final year in the public school system. I counted down the days to graduation.

The end of the year could not come fast enough. I looked forward to never having to sit through another IEP meeting again. An IEP, otherwise known as the Individualized Education Program, is meant to serve as an advocacy initiative for students with special needs. Having a physical disability meant I became one of their candidates. Sounds great, right? I sure didn't think so.

These meetings were a time for teachers, parents, school administrators, and counselors to gather with a disabled student to address their accommodation needs. Besides being unbearably long and boring, the meetings posed a more concerning issue. Instead of being encouraging, they felt off the mark. It seemed as though they were conducted in a fashion opposite of their intended purpose. What really got under my skin was the impression that my weaknesses were highlighted over my strengths.

From elementary to high school, all of my IEP meetings felt this way. There was always a perky counselor, therapist, or administrator telling me what they thought I needed. Instead of giving me a voice, they ignored my perspective and ideas. With every year that passed, my tolerance for the meetings degraded. For this reason, I developed a bit of an attitude and a nonchalant demeanor every time an IEP was convened.

Before my last meeting, I had made up my mind to behave no differently. My mission was to keep a stony expression, act cool, sign papers, and get out of there as soon as possible. Little did I know, this final meeting would have an unforgettable effect on me. It opened my eyes, cut me deep, and challenged my motivation on a level I had never experienced before.

Already frustrated from having to leave my extended lunch period for an IEP meeting, I sat in the counselor's office waiting for my mother to arrive. My eyes stayed on the clock, urging the minute hand faster. As they gathered my files and shuffled papers, the administrators laughed and joked with each other. Besides engaging in some initial small talk with a plastered smile on my face (mom didn't tolerate her daughters being disrespectful to adults), I wasn't interested in conversation.

As they went on and on, talking about changes in the school system, my idle stares into space turned into my personal time to reflect and anticipate my future. Graduation was approaching fast and there was so much left for me to do. Against a backdrop of their incessant chatter, I smirked as I thought about seeing my name on a diploma. *Can't wait to leave these chumps,* I thought to myself. Ask any teenager—completion of high school is more than just a celebrated event with family and friends. In my life, graduation was more than some ever thought I'd accomplish.

**My journey in public school was riddled with ups and downs.
I struggled to be accepted as an ordinary student.
Ironically, students weren't the ones I had problems with.**

My fellow students treated me well. Despite my obvious physical difference, I was admired for my personality and always found myself surrounded by a crew of friends. Adults, however, routinely exacerbated my struggles. They couldn't identify with me, seeing only my differences, and their attempts to shield me from dangers only held me back.

For all of these reasons and more, graduating from high school signified a move to independence, and an exercise of boldness and responsibility. At the closing of this chapter in my life, I could almost taste the sweet freedom of adulthood. And believe it or not, this had been my frame of mind since the moment I entered high school as a thirteen-year-old freshman. Playing a sport, trying out for cheerleading, and taking driver's education were all feats I wanted to tackle, but couldn't.

If anything, I knew my biggest chance to stand out and reach the promised land of graduation day was my academic performance. And if there was one thing I could do, it was hitting the books and excelling in my classes. I was motivated to do well because it was the key to my future.

I dreamed about going to college. When I was a little girl running around with pigtails in my curly brown hair, my mother often told me *the sky was the limit* and that if I did well in school, I could go to college and have any career I wanted.

I held onto that promise, and came to my senior year with not only an exceptional transcript, but a clear vision of what college I wanted to attend. My GPA afforded me the opportunity to pick from many great institutions of higher learning. Although my grades brought me happiness and pride, nothing was more satisfying than the chance to be a student at the college of my choice.

I was fortunate to have an older sister who was already engaging in her studies at the place I wanted to call home for the next four years. Her testament of her experience, my random weekend visits, along with the school's reputation of being a great university, all captured my attention and solidified my desire to attend. The icing on the cake was finding out my best friend was also accepted and planned to attend. I had made up my mind. I wanted to be an Aggie.

My daydreaming about the future was interrupted by the knock at the office door and my mother entering the room. *Good*, I thought. *Now we can get this show on the road!*

The first part of the meeting went exactly as I expected. Greetings. Small talk. Rehashing the old details of the previous meeting. An assessment of accommodations. And finally the segment wherein I shared my future goals. The main topic on their list—college. When asked which colleges I had in mind, I confidently told them I planned to attend North Carolina Agricultural and Technical State University. I had anticipated smiles, encouraging words, or at least a pat on the back. Something to bolster my confidence.

Unfortunately, that wasn't the case. My decision was met with unexpected opposition. None of the adults were particularly thrilled with my college choice. Even my mom had a bit of hesitancy on her face. My thoughts spun. *What is this? They're all acting like I said something wrong.*

My counselor asked, "Well, have you given any other colleges some thought?"

Of course I'd considered other colleges. My city was the home of Wake Forest University, an excellent institution and home distinguished law school that would have made transitioning from undergraduate to graduate easy. But it wasn't where I wanted to be.

"Yeah, but I really like A&T," I explained. "Plus, for my undergraduate career, I thought it would be cool to attend a Historically Black College or University."

Silence.

"Here is the thing," said my counselor. "There's a lot to consider when you choose a college, especially with you needing accommodations for your disability. Just any school may not be suitable for you."

Beneath their soft tone and careful words, I could hear their fear and doubt. At this point, I zoned out and stopped trying to defend myself. Looking back today, I understand that their concerns were not without merit.

North Carolina A&T was a historically black institution. The richness of the campus was due in part to the buildings which has taught and housed generations of African Americans. Despite many challenges—including underfunding, violence ignited by the racial tension of the 1960s, and much more—these buildings withstood the test of time, and were ready yet again to service another generation of students. The strength and the boldness of this institution attracted me, resonating with what I aimed to stand for. Unfortunately, this depth of history also meant that some of the buildings weren't wheelchair accessible. Many of the old dormitories presented the same issue, leading others, including my mother, to second guess my decision to attend.

At such a critical and ambitious time in my life, cautionary words certainly weren't what I wanted to hear. Since birth, I'd been thrown obstacles. I saw the challenges of college as nothing less than the next obstacle to overcome. I was determined to gain the collegiate experience I deserved. Unfortunately, I'd shown up to the meeting with only my desire, lacking the answers or the plan needed to support my decision. All I had was a bag of optimism. I was carrying the hope that my mother gave me.

Even though I felt limitless after achieving academic success, I was encouraged to rethink my dreams.

Etched in my memory forever is the moment a counselor handed me a pamphlet advertising another college, and told it would be my best option for post-secondary education.

"This school will have all the accommodations for students in wheelchairs."

"They have a program for students with disabilities."

"It'll be in your best interest to check it out."

These details were presented to my mother in hopes that she would steer me in this direction. I remained silent for the rest of the meeting, frustrated and fighting to keep from displaying a disrespectful attitude. The whole time, I kept thinking of all of my peers, wondering how many of them had the opportunity to choose where to spend their college years.

To me, being pressured toward an alternative school for fear that I might struggle more at my chosen institution wasn't helpful in the least. In my eyes, it was the alternative choice that actually threatened to hinder me. It would've prevented me from living life the way I wanted, and a denial of everything I had worked so hard for.

The meeting came to a close. I was given a pat on the back and strong encouragement to abandon my college of choice. I left angry and perplexed, already second guessing so much. For the first time, I looked at my future and it didn't seem as bright. *If I'm being encouraged to alter my dreams now, what other dreams will I be told to give up?*

I found my table of friends in the senior area of the lunchroom. I rolled smackdab into the middle of a conversation on the colleges they were considering. They spoke with such excitement and anticipation. The more they talked, the angrier I became, until helpless tears began to roll down my face. Everyone at the table quickly took notice and begged for an explanation. Embarrassed, I shrugged it off and said I was okay.

But the longer the tears fell, the more empowered I became.

Strength and determination increased with every salty drop. Every limitation, every bad diagnosis, every barrier that was ever placed on my life, came rushing into my mind. By the time the bell rang for us to return to class, I was fired up and ready to go. Ready to attack my dream and soar into my destiny.

•••

This situation isn't the only major obstacle I've had to endure. I've had plenty. But something about that meeting really broke the camel's back of my hard-won optimism. In hindsight, it was a back that needed to be broken. That trial gave me the drive required to adamantly and fiercely tackle any challenge in my life, even those that presented as too hard to overcome. The passion birthed that day came with labor pains, but brought forth something that could never be stolen from me. I was given my *WHY*, and was pointed to the path of my purpose.

Today, I am convinced that the journey to success cannot be completed without a reason and appreciation for the work you're doing. Perhaps there's a scenario, situation, or special person in your life serving as the fuel behind your drive. Something has to ignite a fire in you and be substantial enough to keep the fire burning. Without such a catalyst, it's easy to become careless or irresponsible.

Being in an adverse position can diminish your ability to see the light at the end of a tunnel. Without ambition, quitting becomes an option, and you might never experience the incredible life you're meant to have. Therefore, if you have a desire to be effective and fulfilled, you must find your personal *WHY*.

The Will to Succeed

Several years ago, the importance of having a *WHY* became even more meaningful. I found out that having a purpose and a sense of belonging can literally mean life or death for an individual.

After a long day working third shift at one of the major hospitals in our city, my sister came home stressed and downtrodden. Noticing the strain on her face and in her body language, I asked her what was wrong. She shared with me how difficult it was to see patients in her care fighting illnesses alone, without family or friends for support.

"There are too many people suffering and dying alone," she told me. "Where are the families who will give these patients the will to live?" Her response was not exactly what I anticipated. But her concern peaked my interest.

The will to live. A profound statement that led me to want to learn more. To my surprise, a few minutes of research revealed that a Will to Live is an actual psychological force that drives you toward a more positive state of being. When faced with the threat of death, many individuals, whether consciously or unconsciously, fight harder to stay alive if they believe there's something worth living for. For this reason, professionals in the medical field encourage the support and visitation of family members during their patients' times of poor health.

Studies have shown that with the care and encouragement of loved ones, patients pursue healing with much more determination. The reason? The patient now has a *WHY* to motivate them. The same is true for an individual looking to soar in life.

Put simply, your *WHY* is your will to succeed. So before you invest any time or energy pursuing success, ask yourself, *What is my* WHY? Capture it. Identify it. Don't find yourself among those who work without any purpose fueling their actions.

Operating without a clear vision of what lies at the finish line is the quickest way to disappointment, confusion, and a mediocre life.

I often ask myself why I possess such a need to help others soar. But the more I interact with others, the more evident the answer becomes. Look around you and consider this: Have you ever seen someone stuck in a mundane routine, unable to break free or experience spontaneity and growth?

I see it every day. From conversations with individuals at speaking engagements, to scrolling down my Facebook timeline, I see an overload of unhappy or dissatisfied people. And nine times out of ten, the reason the person is living a defeated life is because they're merely existing, without any understanding of why.

They haven't yet assigned meaning to that three letter word – *WHY* – and experienced how it can give their life direction. Finding a *WHY* isn't as hard as you might think; inspiration is all around us. My favorite place to renew my purpose is in the presence of children. It is rather spectacular that in the midst of such a progressive society full of adults who claim to know it all, children have an unlimited desire to discover truths about life. The word *WHY* holds so much value to them.

I can attest to this, as I'm constantly posed with the question of *WHY* by little ones. My conversations with children are typically interspersed with questions derived from their curiosity. Questions pertaining to my life or physical makeup always seem to surface, and are quite entertaining. Yet make no mistake, children never settle for a quick answer. With that little wheel spinning in their heads, eyebrows raised, and shy stutter, they always follow up with *why*. It amazes me every time.

You see, even children understand that having explanations for results is important. For without the question of *why,* we would all remain in the dark. Which, sadly, is the case for many people. But pinpointing your personal *WHY* has an opposite effect, bringing light to the darkness. Your *WHY* will liberate you, and give you both the permission and the authority to act accordingly toward a desired result.

From the countless, fascinating conversations I've had with children, all the way back to that transformative IEP meeting, finding my *WHY* has fundamentally changed my perspective in life. A forty-five-minute meeting became a major contributor to my purpose. From the hurt and the pain of that experience was birthed a gift so bright that no one could ever diminish it.

I didn't know it at the time, but now that I look back over my life I realize that in that moment I wanted more for myself than what was being offered by a system and a society that didn't understand me. It propelled me to develop confidence in my God-given gifts, and alleviated all my fears about the struggles ahead. From then on, I had the self-assurance and audacity to go after anything I wanted. And that's what I did, starting with boldly going against the grain and attending the college of my choice. Was it risky? Absolutely. But it gave me even more purpose.

Rolling across the stage four years later and graduating college with high honors ultimately shifted my mindset away from self-centeredness. My *WHY* was developing and blossoming right before my eyes, and I wanted to tell everybody that they, too, could soar to great heights.

The more I accomplished in my own life, the more I wanted to help others achieve greatness. From that seed of positivity grew my ambition and strength; conversely, my fear began to wither.

When my *WHY* shifted and evolved, I grew brave enough to declare more for my life.

After graduating college, I said to myself, *I've made it this far, I might as well go big or go home…* and law school was a BIG for me. Opening my acceptance letter and reading that the law school of *my choice* wanted me was overwhelming. I laid in the middle of my living room floor overcome with confidence and happiness.

I felt like I was on the brink of a major undertaking, one that was never promised to me but was proof that anything was possible. Again I asked myself, *Monique, what's your WHY?* Was it about proving people wrong? Speaking transparently, heck yes. Part of it was. Pumped with all the self-confidence running through my veins, I wanted to shut the mouth of fear and smash limitations with my little hands. The other part of my *WHY* was that law school would afford me the opportunity to impact individuals on a greater scale.

Today, I shake my head in awe at how one IEP meeting both ignited an undying spark inside me. Now, I have an obligation to ensure that my family members, friends, community, and beyond hear my story, and walk away knowing that nothing can hold them back.

• • •

Everyone has a story, and yours might very well be the motivation behind your desire to achieve. For some it may be a loved one, someone who prayed for you during tough times, or a child who depends on you to show them the way. It could even be an individual in your community that you don't know, but for whom you have a deep appreciation. Or maybe you experienced poverty as a child and vowed to never experience it again.

There are so many reasons, so many causes that can motivate you on your journey. Know your *WHY*. Remember your *WHY*. It will help you stay committed to your journey. Be able, willing, and unashamed to articulate your personal purpose. Expressing the basis of your motivation will have a positive ripple effect on those around you.

A lot of people who have reached the pinnacle of success neglect to share what pushed them forward in life. But sharing your *WHY* will put people on notice and educate others as to what you're all about. Success without a story or a purpose is hollow and unfulfilling. Hollow success does not produce meaningful substance.

By now, I hope you're thinking about your *WHY*. What does it mean to you? Not knowing your *WHY* and coming up empty-handed when asked can be disheartening. You may think, *I don't know why I do the things I do.* Or maybe you don't know how to articulate why you do what you do. Maybe all you know is that you have a goal and you're trying to reach it. That's okay! Simply having the desire to find your *WHY* is enough to get the process started.

Don't stress yourself out by trying to quickly come up with something. On the other hand, there may be some of you thinking, *Is it really so hard to find a why in my life?* For some people, the answer is yes. It can be difficult to pinpoint a *WHY* if you feel like you've always been drowning in despair and haven't had an opportunity to come up for air. You may feel like you don't have a *WHY* worth sharing, or one worth being the gasoline to fuel your fire.

• • •

Whatever the opposition preventing you from finding your *WHY*, consider looking at your life and reflecting on the questions below. Write your feelings and answers down in an organic, raw fashion. Don't worry about the opinions of others. Pinpoint what gets you hyped in life. That is the best way to generate an authentic reference to your story. Your *WHY* isn't only what supports your purpose, but what links your identity with your passion.

LET'S SOAR!

What moment, time period, or condition provokes you to do and have more. What serves as the spoon stirring the passion in your life?

_____

_____

_____

_____

_____

_____

Now try to correlate that conjuring of passion with your dreams. What does your dream life look like?

_____

_____

_____

_____

_____

_____

How do they connect? Why do they connect?

_____

_____

_____

_____

LESSON TWO

Who Are You Connected To?

> WHETHER YOU'RE JUST STARTING OUT ON YOUR JOURNEY OR A WELL-SEASONED TRAVELER, AT NO POINT SHOULD YOU RISK YOUR DREAMS ON SOMEONE WHO DOESN'T REPRESENT GREATNESS.

@madetwosoar

Birds of a Feather

If you have a mother like mine, I'm sure you've heard this phrase before: "Birds of a feather flock together." During my years as a teen, it seemed as though every authoritative figure wanted to preach these words to young people. My parents, in all of their wisdom, understood the truth of this statement. They understood it so well that while I lived under their roof, they shamelessly pried into my social life to make sure this little bird wasn't flying with the wrong crew.

Coming up in the 90s, my sisters and I didn't have the luxury of smartphones and social media. Of course, there were still ways to be sneaky, but my parents were very clever. If we were talking on the phone, they could easily pick up in another room of the house, cover the receiver, and have a listen. The only way to be sure no one else was on the line was to click over. If I heard a dial tone, the coast was clear and I was free to say whatever I wanted.

But my parents didn't need to listen in on our conversations to know what was going on in our lives. Endowed with an uncanny awareness, they knew by our behavior when the quality of our social circles had changed. If we were slacking in our schoolwork, engaging in increased conflict with each other as siblings, or even using new slang words, we could expect my mom to be on us like white on rice. She would want to know the cause of the change. And even though we were growing and evolving as young ladies, she knew our cores. Mom knew our natural tendencies, our different personalities, but more importantly, she knew of the high standard by which we were raised.

So she never hesitated to ask what was going on with us when we seemed a little out of whack. A majority of the time, we didn't tell her outright. The most she'd receive from us was a shrug or a muttered, "Nothing."

"Who you been hanging around?" was the question that usually followed.

The question always irked me and sent my eyes rolling to the back of my head (such a disrespectful gesture was certainly not done in her view). I wanted to shout, "What does that have to do with anything?" but I knew better. My parents were loving but strict. Raising me and my sisters in a heavily influential environment of rambunctious neighborhood kids, they were never lenient regarding the company we kept. Because my parents were firm, I knew that if I mentioned any one of my friends, mom would automatically determine that I must've been negatively influenced by them. And once a friend was on my parent's bad list, it was virtually impossible to convince them they didn't belong there.

Birds of a feather flock together. Today, this saying is more than just a phrase for me. Quite frankly, it has been a safety precaution and a dream-saver. It's a reminder that everything that I do, and even who I am connected to, affects my accomplishments in life. In a way, it has also established within me the framework of what it means to be socially responsible—a practice that alludes to just how powerful each individual is and can be. My behavior, acted in both a conscious and subconscious manner, influences others. At the same time, the behavior of others affects me, which is why it's essential to remind myself of the phrase when I'm making choices in my social life.

I didn't quite understand it as a youngster, but as I stepped into adulthood, I realized that if I desired a particular outcome in life, it was in my best interest to see this outcome reflected by those surrounding me. For example, if I want peace and tranquility, being around peaceful and harmonious people is highly beneficial. If I want to live a healthier lifestyle, interacting, exercising, and sharing mealtimes with friends who also prioritize healthy living does me good. If there are times I find myself bogged down by life circumstances, hanging around friends who are free, spontaneous, and lighthearted is a haven.

I am less worried about being socially accepted, and more focused on finding, developing, and valuing healthy relationships.

This focus comes at the price of being vigilant and constantly raising the bar regarding those I connect with. My method of choosing the right friends has come through trial and error, and has certainly been laced with experiences and individuals I wish I had dodged.

When it comes to friendships and social bonds, my most shocking and disheartening experiences have been dealing with unreliable, downtrodden, and unfocused people. These occurrences blew my mind and left me questioning the moral compasses of some of my so-called friends. Can you relate? I'm sure you can. I wouldn't be surprised if you're thinking about people you are connected to who fit the same mold.

If you're completely honest with yourself, the thought of your connection to them may even make you uneasy. Well, great! It should. Because the truth is, the negative energy and attributes of others will have an effect on your life, and it's not a good one. In the previous chapter, we learned that success takes time. The journey is long and I believe you'd agree—you could do without extra bumps in the road.

Dodging those bumps by decreasing your involvement in poor relationships means you've got some work to do on your current social circle. Your circle needs to be restructured.

But how do you restructure the group of people you are most connected to? One step at a time. One *bold* step at time. How bold? Well, you've got to realize that oftentimes, the same people you know to be unmotivated and untrustworthy are the very same individuals with whom you've grown stagnant. It can be hard to admit, but they are often the same people who have represented the norm for you because you've chalked their behavior up to, *That's just the way they are.*

Sometimes, these relationships can be the most disheartening because they may involve the people you love and call family. That's when it really stings. When it's people you care about creating negativity in your life, it makes shifting your circle much harder. That's why you must approach such reconstruction intentionally, with a clear mind and a plan in place.

The Character Test

So now you're thinking about switching up your circle to represent the best team you can have at this point in your life. But where do you start? The first step in changing your connections is to commit to the process. Committing requires you adopt a new mindset, one unhindered by fear or complacency. To be successful, approach the process with deliberate, unwavering honesty.

Gone are the days of making excuses for people's behavior, lifestyles, or shortcomings. You simply don't have to deal with them. Instead, you must deal with you. Gaining a positively influencing circle of friends requires you to be truthful about whom you associate with now and why.

If we are to decipher the types of people we engage with, one of the best ways is to determine their character. Character is a person's mental, moral, and perhaps spiritual qualities. One of my most helpful tools to determine character is what I call a Character Test. With a simple objective and process, the test only becomes challenging when we are not honest or dedicated enough to making changes.

The Character Test places you as the evaluator and your friends and associates under evaluation. In your role as the evaluator, know that you are in control. You call the shots. Only you know how much reaching your dreams means to you. You bear the responsibility of making your dreams a reality.

Take the time to consider the individuals you share yourself with. It may take one session of brainstorming, or you may want to take a week to really consider the people in your life. Collect the names of these individuals. Call them out, bring them to the forefront of your mind and write them down.

- Think about your coworkers.
- What about the people you go to lunch with?
- Perhaps study partners?
- Who are you dating?
- Who do you consider your mentor?

Make sure that none of the people you voluntarily spend time with are left off the list. Now, allow yourself a few minutes to review the names. Each person on your list, whether they are good or bad influences, brings something to the table. Who are you inviting to your table of life?

Sharing space and time with someone means you likely also share your thoughts, dreams, and heart with them. These are some of the most coveted, meaningful aspects of a person. Take another look at your list. These are the individuals you are allowing to partake in the most invaluable aspects of your being. Sounds a bit intimate? It is. Especially when you place high value on your life and ideas.

Heighten your awareness of who you are involved with. Because the truth is, not everyone is equipped or qualified to support your dreams. It may not be through any fault of their own. But not everyone can accept you and where you are in this season of your life. The sooner you're able to recognize those misplaced individuals, the quicker you can render CPR to the dreams that were being choked by their negativity.

So what does a character evaluation look like? I've found it helpful to set a criterion for those in my inner circle. If you don't meet this criterion, you won't partake in my life's adventures. This might sound restrictive or excessive. But it's neither. It's about being clear and concise and not compromising on what you truly need.

In the same regard, your standard for friendships should not be guided by shallow constructs such as status, money, or physical attributes. These factors have no effect on the integrity, sincerity, or personality of a person, and don't determine authenticity.

I have worked with some extremely wealthy individuals who have never experienced financial woes, but sadly, lack the ability to communicate respectfully. And I have been blessed by some who from their outward appearance don't seem to have much to offer, but who possessed wealth in knowledge and compassion. The criterion for those you build relationships with should surpass a mediocre standard. You are worthy of connecting with people who embody excellence and can provide the type of companionship you desire.

Character Test: Four Questions to Ask.

1. **What do they bring to our relationship that makes me a better person?**

    Never showing up at a party empty handed has been a practice of mine for years. Whenever someone is gracious enough to invite me to an event, one of the first questions I ask after checking my schedule and considering whether I'd like to attend is, "Do you need me to bring anything?" Whether it's a lovely gift or a bag of potato chips, my offering represents my effort to add value wherever my presence is requested.

With my contribution in hand, my hope is that my personality will also bring joy, positive vibes, and most importantly significance. Your relationships with the people in your life should be the same way. This is not to say that relationships won't have natural ups and downs. Some days will be better than others. Yet overall, two parties in a relationship should be enjoying it. I've made this a requirement in my own life, as I strive to cultivate positivity and an abundance of joy.

Key requirements for being a part of my circle include having good communication skills, genuine engagement, and a desire to uplift others. If these characteristics are missing, then in my book the relationship is useless. We are either declining in status or remaining the same. Surprisingly, there are some who don't mind staying the same. Not me. Remaining stagnant in a situation that requires growth to be effective is dysfunctional.

To obtain a functioning circle of friends, be sure you're selecting your connections for their ability to both teach and learn from you. When you align with another in this fashion, over time you'll experience a strengthening of your weaknesses.

Doubtlessly, some of your past mistakes could have been avoided or processed more effectively with the support of a good friend. And this is just the tip of the iceberg regarding the benefits a good connection can render. As you push toward your goals, utilize your instinct to determine who to add to your inner circle, and who might be hindering your success.

Try to imagine a table for two, where the table is the foundation of a friendship. What kind of fruit does your friend bring to the table? See, fruit represents the attributes, skills, knowledge, and personality type of a person. Sometimes the wrong people possess fruit that is not for you to consume. Be wise and resist the impulse to take a bite. Without your thorough inspection, you may fall to friends who will sit back and watch you partake of their rotten fruit. But a good friend brings forth good fruit in the right season of your life. If they are a nurturing, enriching influence in your life, what they bear will be of value to you.

2. **Does this person have an honorable reputation, one I strive to acquire?**

In the world of business, reputation means everything. If you want to try a new restaurant, you likely seek out reviews prior to making your reservation. When my schedule permits, I love to sit in front of the big screen at my local theater and enjoy a good movie. But nowadays, a movie trailer on television isn't enough incentive for me to go to the theater. Before I spend money on a ticket and popcorn, I do a little investigation, reading reviews and ratings from movie critics. What I seek is raw, honest feedback from those who've seen the movie. Whether or not I spend my money comes down to the informed perspectives of my peers. Every business owner should understand the importance of upholding a good reputation with their supporters, observers, and clients.

When I first became interested in creating and sharing Made 2 Soar with others, I envisioned a brand and an initiative that would connect with my future audience in a positive way. When people want to invest time, money, or any other resource, they generally consider factors such as reputation, quality, and what the company or business stands for. Why? Because people don't want to involve themselves with something they don't agree with.

We can easily apply these same principles to vetting the people who make up our circle. With the gigantic popularity and accessibility of social media, we have each become our own brand, posted for all to evaluate. With platforms such as Facebook, Instagram, Snapchat, and Twitter, it's easy to size someone up by simply reviewing their social media content. No longer do you have to rely on what someone else says about a person. You don't even have to hear it through the "grapevine." Social media tells it all, and will often give you all you need to make a determination of a person's character. It's amazing how many account holders use social media like an open diary, revealing their personality, habits, and shifting moods.

Let's face it, people air way too much of their personal business on social media. But I use it to my advantage. If you're like me, and desire to be around great people, these are the platforms that can help you easily assess a person's reputation. Take advantage of social media to avoid developing unhealthy attachments. Listen to your instinct. If someone posts something that makes you uncomfortable, or contradicts your way of life, listen to that inner warning system. Such an unfavorable connection has the potential to clip your wings, negatively influencing you, and bringing confusion to others who are on the outside looking in. All of a sudden, your observers start to associate you with the poor character of the person you hang around. Is that a fair assessment? Maybe not. But I say err on the side of caution.

Your inner circle of support is so important that even I become very risk-averse regarding this area in my both personal and business arenas. Your reputation should be a cherished treasure. Having a good one is rare in today's society of liars, deceivers, and thieves. Your reputation can make or break you. Whether you're just starting out on your journey or a well-seasoned traveler, at no point should you risk your dreams on someone who doesn't represent greatness.

3. Am I an asset to this person?
    Good relationships consist of continuous give-and-take.

When we are searching for new connections, we often look for people who can assist in our own endeavors. We seek those who can invest, grow, and refine our ideas, businesses, and status. However, we sometimes do this without considering the consequences. Before we know it, word on the street or in the office is that we're a taker, a leech, or helpless. These are difficult labels to remove from the memory bank of others.

Don't be the one others avoid because you're perceived as a liability. If you find yourself in this position, you might be thinking, *I am not a liability; I stay busy making my dreams come true.* Unfortunately, we don't always realize our own problematic conduct, especially when we're clawing our way through adversity to the top of our own mountain.

Although it's easy to adopt a "by any means necessary" approach, the relationships you establish shouldn't be based on this premise. Know yourself. Take inventory of behaviors and habits that might cause your relationships to be off-balanced, skewing them in the direction of your needs. Be honest and consider whether you're treating your connections the way you'd like to be treated. If you feel like you've fallen short, it's never too late to turn around and began rebuilding your inner circle.

Take a few moments to consider the needs and dreams of others. What gifts, talents or interests do you have that can be of use to someone else? How can you help improve the lives of your friends and family members?

Serving as an asset to someone doesn't mean you're a doormat. An asset is valuable because of its worth. As you serve as an asset, make sure you are not simultaneously diminishing your own worth. Making a difference in the life of another should make a difference in your life, as well.

4. **Are we sharpening and enriching each other's personality, skills, or knowledge?**

It serves me well to see those I'm connected to improving and progressing along with me. My heart is overjoyed when the people I care about are defeating personal strongholds and challenges that threaten their well-being. Some of the most meaningful relationships consist of two people who find pleasure in benefiting others and who are not afraid to be sharpened. As you are searching for the right people to share space with, consider whether an individual has skills or knowledge that will elevate your own abilities or comprehension. Can you do the same for them?

There is always more value in building with two sharpened minds versus one.

These are simple questions that will help guide your thinking during this process. As the evaluator, there may be other questions you want to add to help you make the right decisions. If so, great! Have at it. The whole idea here is for you to determine your personal connections based on your perception and honest assessment.

The Character Test questions give you the authority to dictate what's best for you. The answers don't have to be long or complicated. A simple *Yes* or *No* may do. Don't compromise on truth by giving long explanations that turn into excuses. We are not evaluating a person's single good day or weakness. Instead, we are looking at the totality of the person's value in your life. It's not about judging, but about surrounding yourself with people who compliment you.

Once you've completed your assessments, it's time to begin the work. Every name should find its place in one of these categories: "Move On" or "Remain Friends." Make a determination for every name on your list. The titles of the categories above are self-explanatory, and offer guidance on how to progress in each current relationship. You can either move on from a person or remain friends, permitting them to continue growing with you.

When you have finalized your categories, it's time to fully accept the results. Accepting the results means becoming comfortable with decreasing your involvement with those in the "Move On" category. This task can be tough. But as difficult as it may be, do not stay on this step too long. The longer it takes for you to accept the results, the more you will begin to second-guess what's best for you.

If you've completed these first steps thoroughly, wholeheartedly, and honestly, the results are an accurate evaluation. Trust your instinct and stand firm in your decisions.

Detaching From Toxic Relationships

When I decided to do my first assessment, my struggle was not wrestling with who should be a part of my life and who shouldn't. Acting on my decisions was a far more daunting task. *What would people say when I stopped talking to them? How would people feel if they knew they were on the "Move On" list?* With these questions circling in my head, my judgment became cloudy, and I became increasingly focused on the feelings of others. In turn, I sacrificed my own feelings. I just didn't want to let anyone down! I became anxious, worried, and even disappointed in myself.

My confidence returned, however, when I formulated exit plans. Everyone's personality is different. There may be some people you'll have no problem separating yourself from. But take another look at your "Move On" list. Perhaps there are a couple of names that you know having an exit plan for will help you take action and follow through. For some, an upfront and clear-cut disconnection is appropriate. That could be the only way a person will understand how deeply committed you are to changing your life. For others, making mild adjustments to the relationship will suffice. For example, you may decrease your availability to hang out with them socially. Or perhaps you refrain from engaging in negative conversations with them.

These small adjustments can speak volumes, and will help you manifest the right relationships in your life.

Although it can be a tough process, here are a few tips for severing toxic relationships.

1. **Focus less on them and their issues. Make this about you and your destiny.**

   Individuals on your "Move On" list are there because of their behavior, or lack thereof. Regardless, resist playing the blame game. Instead of focusing on their liabilities, stay focused on your future. Part of the reason why it can seem so difficult to detach is because you're worried that your actions are unethical, or that you're the villain.

   Detaching yourself from an individual does not involve you putting down, bashing, or operating disrespectfully. It can be done with tact. The best thing you can do—not only for yourself but for someone else—is to discontinue a relationship that is not producing good fruits. You are in control of your destiny. And that means you can no longer rely on the failures, inadequacies, and unreliability of others as excuses for where you are in life.

2. **Remember, your time is invaluable.**

   A wonderful exit strategy that I've implemented often is minimizing the time I spend with those I'm disconnecting from. I've simply become a better steward of how, and with whom, I spend my time. No longer do I allow myself to be consumed or influenced by people who don't belong in my life.

Time is a precious commodity. Once wasted, absolutely no one can get it back. Only God can recreate or replenish time. If you look at the grand scheme of life, you will realize that we have but a short time on this earth. Every day, every minute, and every second counts, and should be dedicated to becoming the best individual possible. And you cannot be your best self by spending time with the wrong people.

3. **Set Boundaries.**

Setting boundaries is also a great exit strategy. Especially if you aren't comfortable with a more direct approach. Cultivating better relationships calls for the phasing out of poor ones. Boundaries allow you to determine what you will tolerate, as well as how involved you'd like to be with an individual. Clear, concise boundaries will decrease the stress of detachment because you are operating purposefully.

Your boundaries ought to reflect your values and aspirations. If integrity, honesty, and trustworthiness are what you respect and want attached to your reputation, expect the same from those in your social circle. Consequently, it may become necessary to only engage in conversations and behavior that are uplifting and edifying. Conversations involving gossip and dishonesty should become off-limits. This boundary is a foolproof way to weed out negative influences in your life.

Be mindful and prepared. Your boundaries will be tested. Stand firm, and don't allow the opinions of toxic people to distract you from your mission.

Setting boundaries allows you to act autonomously, building confidence while helping you act intentionally.

Show Yourself Friendly

We are highly complicated, emotionally driven beings. Because we are all dependent on other humans in some form or fashion, it's no wonder attachments are so hard to break, and new ones hard to form.

But I tell you, greatness is birthed from a healthy and fulfilling relationship. In order to find friends, you must be friendly. This profound truth has the power not only to reshape and renew current relationships, but generate new, deeply meaningful connections.

First, you must be willing to receive and maintain healthy connections, and be in a position to do so. Positioning yourself requires being in the right place at the right time. This doesn't mean you will always be able to predict how or when you'll meet the right people; however, if you go places where your desired connections are more likely to be, you increase the probability of starting meaningful relationships.

It can be difficult to align ourselves with exceptional individuals if we continue to wallow in mediocrity.

Do you find it difficult to make friends in the places you fellowship? Step outside where you typically socialize and explore other arenas. Observe what you learn and the people you learn from. Remember, being friendly implies willingness to build new relationships.

One of the most prominent ways in which we hinder ourselves is viewing our current situation through the lens of past experiences. A lot of times, we are so damaged and hurt by failed relationships that we don't allow room for new vibrations and gratifying connections. Don't burden yourself by continuing to suffer over what happened in the past. Every poor relationship you've endured can work in your favor if, and only if, you choose to learn from them.

My first year of college pinpoints a time in my life wherein I truly realized that the quality of my circle of friends mattered. Living on such a populated campus, where I constantly interacted with other students, I learned the importance of conducting evaluations of my connections. The more evaluations I conducted, the more I began to decipher and identify the attributes of individuals I did not prefer, did not bond with, and should simply avoid.

The evaluations were tough because they were eye openers for me. As I made my lists and stared back at the names, I was literally coming face-to-face with people I had allowed to steal my joy. While I should have been rejoicing at the chance to filter out negativity, I was let down by my lack of discernment in choosing friends.

A few days went by before the truth hit me. Never feel bad about your experiences in life! Some relationships may not be deemed worthwhile in the long run, but the lessons you learn from them are. Those pitfalls matured me and prepared me for the future I wanted. I gained an understanding of people and habits, and how the two can either create wonder or a monster. I share this to encourage you. Your failed friendships should not scare you or impede your progress, but should be the platform from which you soar.

If you stay fearful of your past, you will never be strong enough for your future.

Acquire the right position and mindset. As mentioned, positioning is about being in the right place, but it's also about your mind and heart mirroring those of the people you want to connect with. Do not simply think that people will come to you. Many times it's the opposite.

You attract what you reflect. Sometimes, you just have to show up and deliver. You want to achieve success? Involve yourself with the right, successful people. You may not know these individuals immediately, but as you seek out and evaluate the attributes of successful friends, ask yourself, are you reflecting these same features? Are you showing yourself to be friendly?

Building the Right Circle

Since we've now pointed out ways to disengage from the folks that aren't for us, it's time to soar into the type of people we *should* be involved with. A great circle of friends includes people who exemplify the characteristics of being supportive towards others, and who are successful themselves.

Do we really need friends? Certainly. Life isn't meant to be experienced alone, and the right friends will bring out the best in you while you're on your journey. You're probably wondering, *What do these magical friends look like?* The beauty is that there's no magic at all. Keep your senses and heart wide open, and you'll spot the following characteristics of a great friend.

The Delightfuls

When creating your circle, it's important to have friends who are enjoyable to be around. Sounds so simple, eh? You'd be surprised how many people, when seeking out friends, choose clout, fame, and status over amiability. Our society's glorification of these qualities has wired some of us to gravitate towards things that really don't matter.

So many people are stuck in relationships, friendships, and partnerships with people they don't like. Because of an idolized attribute, they stay, holding on to an undesirable relationship. Their hope is that someday the relationship will elevate their own success.

Positivity and compatibility are key, but you don't have to be cut from the same cloth. In my own life, I'm proud to say that my friends come from many different backgrounds, occupations, personal philosophies, and journeys. No matter the superficial differences between you, a true friend—someone you can trust and who uplifts you—is invaluable.

Look for characteristics that mean something to you. For example, as a person who values humor, I look for friends who don't mind letting their hair down every once in a while to engage in a bit of comedy. Laughter releases endorphins, a powerful chemical that can empower an individual to seek out the best in life—the type of sensation that will keep you smiling and enjoying your path to success. Pleasant people are not a drag to be around, and allow you to feel both confident and lighthearted at once.

The Equippers

Secondly, align yourself with people that I call "Equippers." Equippers are willing to share their expertise and wisdom with you. Kind and thoughtful, they help equip you with the necessary tools to reach your goals.

No matter how confident you are in your abilities, or how accomplished you've become, never be a know-it-all. Remain teachable by aligning yourself with someone who is more competent and knowledgeable than you in your respective field. Coming into contact with the right equippers may require a bit of searching.

Be neither dismayed nor surprised by the selfishness of some who hold knowledge, but are unwilling to educate others. Sadly, many individuals who have "reached the top" have fallen prey to their egos. Being "self-made" and "independent" can become so important that we forget the value in showing our brothers and sisters the way. As a result, many aggressively tear down others to reach the pinnacle of success. Truly accomplished individuals, however, understand that growing, giving, receiving, and learning are essential for success.

During every phase of your life you will need someone to help equip you for the next level. Where are they? Who do you look for? You may have an awesome boss, professor, spiritual mentor, or elderly person in your life who fits the bill of an Equipper. Hone in on those who have stored-up wisdom and possess the key to unlocking your next adventure. Seek them. Invite them into your circle with humility and a willingness to be taught.

The Encouragers

Encouragers are a special group, its members often difficult to find. So when you come across someone who fits in this category, grab them! Now, don't physically grab them and scare them off. What I mean is that you should appreciate them, and express your sincere need for their presence in your life. Encouragers can be the fuel in your engine. Life is hard; there is no doubt about it. You will experience times when success seems like an unobtainable dream. There have been plenty of days in my life when quitting felt like an easy and acceptable escape from struggle.

In fact, strangers who only see my exterior might assume I have good reasons to throw in the towel. I can't tell you how many strangers have noticed my disability, and approached me to say these five, dreaded words: "I feel sorry for you."

The first couple of times it happens, you dismiss it and consider that maybe they have lost a few marbles. But after hearing it several times, your faith becomes a little vulnerable. Talk about having to be mentally and emotionally strong enough to not run over toes with my wheelchair! While you may not have a physical disability like me, I'm sure developing mental and emotional strength sometimes feels impossible.

There will be challenges in your life that seem insurmountable. And if you're anything like me, you'll try to push forward as much as you can by yourself. Perhaps you'll give yourself pep talks, or a pat on the back once in a while to keep your spirits high.

But there will come a time—many times—when you'll need to be encouraged and uplifted by someone else. Someone who can see your value and appreciate you even when you cannot appreciate yourself. Encouragers help you see the light at the end of the tunnel. They motivate you to tackle even the most difficult obstacles. They will also be the ones who share their unreserved happiness when you succeed.

Most importantly, true Encouragers pray for you even when they are not around. They're always thinking of ways to help you feel better about life, yourself, and where you're going. An Encourager only wants to see you succeed, and harbors no envy. Everyone should be blessed enough to have an Encourager in their corner who is unwavering, honest, and 100% real.

Building the right circle of friends takes time. While it can be tempting to stay in stagnant relationships, stay the course.

**You are valuable and so are your goals and aspirations.
Your connections should exemplify this.**

I can't stress enough that as you seek to define the right circle of friends, never allow status, looks, or money to be the criteria by which you select people. The beauty of developing new friendships is that they can be both sporadic and unpredictable. Who knows? You may help an elderly neighbor carry their groceries inside, and as you do so, they drop serious wisdom into your consciousness. Without seizing the opportunity to be of service, you might never have shared space with them, and would have missed out.

Foremost, evaluate a person's character. Consider how they can positively impact your thinking and improve your work in this world. No matter how old someone is, what they look like, or what they have, the types of people listed above are the rare jewels that will make your life undeniably rich.

LET'S SOAR!

Reflecting on the content of this chapter, jot down three strategies that you can implement in your life to help you choose your social circle.

1. _____

   _____

   _____

   _____

   _____

2. _____

   _____

   _____

   _____

   _____

3. _____

   _____

   _____

   _____

   _____

Who are the Delightfuls, Equippers, and Encouragers in your life?

Delightfuls:

_____

_____

_____

_____

Equippers:

_____

_____

_____

_____

Encouragers:

_____

_____

_____

_____

How can/do you show your appreciation to them?

_____

_____

_____

_____

_____

Soaring involves being aware of any object interference that might hinder your flight. Take a look at your lists above. Are you lacking support in any category? If so, make it known below, along with the intent to identify and adopt new friends who are Delightfuls, Equippers, or Encouragers.

_____

_____

_____

_____

_____

LESSON THREE

Exercising Patience is The Key

"

THOSE WHO FOCUS ON THE GREATER PICTURE AREN'T EASILY DISTRACTED BY THE SWIFT PROGRESSION OF OTHERS AROUND THEM. THEY STAY THEIR COURSE, CONFIDENT AS TO WHERE THEY ARE HEADED.

"

@madetwosoar

How wonderful would it be to wake up tomorrow morning and realize that all your dreams, ambitions, and goals have come to fruition. Just like that. In an instant, you are where you thought you would be in five years. Imagine it.

Perhaps the night prior, you were stressing about your biology test. Then BAM! The next morning you walk into your big, beautiful office and out of the corner of your eye, you notice something on your wall that wasn't there before. It's your degree, nicely matted and framed, hanging there looking dignified. Or maybe you're the owner of a cupcake shop that, in spite of your use of grandma's delicious recipe, is on the verge of closing. Yet the next day, your shop miraculously comes alive, and you open your doors to a line of customers wrapped around your building.

Oh how wondrous it would be if you were teleported to the future and dropped into the perfect life you always imagined. The life you believe you deserve, complete with all the relationships, prestige, and peace you've ever wanted.

If you're human, I can tell you that you've wished for this more than a few times. Living with instant access to our desires is the type of life we crave. This is how swiftly we wish time would pass regarding the very things we want. We value instant gratification. We want what we want and we want it quickly. Fast food, microwaved dinner, electronic responses, text messaging, and emails are just a fraction of the luxuries we enjoy that make our lives easier. We incorporate these features into our lives to simplify, condense, and minimize our efforts in order to get the maximum benefits.

Although I indulge in many modern conveniences myself, I can't help but to also consider how they might be affecting our ability to manage expectations and live fulfilling lives. On the one hand, this new age of technology is exciting and intriguing, yet on the other, it's very telling of how little we are willing to wait for our desires to be satisfied.

But maybe this is to be expected. After all, impatience has woven itself into the DNA of our customs and has even found its way into some of our most sacred and meaningful traditions. And nothing says tradition like the good old holidays we've been celebrating for generations. Yes, impatience has even tainted our reverence of important holidays. For example, as a kid, Christmas was like hitting the lottery overnight. An elaborately decorated tree hovered over my gifts, all of which I would tear open and enjoy having not invested any time or effort toward receiving them. All it took was the clock striking 6:00 a.m. All my dreams would come true on Christmas morning. Instant gratification.

You hear all the time of how Rome wasn't built in a day. But I guarantee it would have been if the Romans could have made it so. From the historical days of Adam and Eve to now, mankind has struggled with patience, as well as the desire to take matters into our own hands. But no one is exempt from the temptation of this pit, including me.

From my days as a young kid ripping open Christmas presents to the adult entrepreneur who is constantly tempted to take the road less-challenged, I have an enormous amount of experience wanting to satisfy my needs quickly. Interestingly, it is my natural tendency to operate expeditiously. Call it the New Yorker in me, but I've never minded running the rat race if the end result got me to my cheese quickly.

Because honestly, who finds pleasure in waiting? Hardly anyone. And even when we are okay with waiting, it's usually because we have placated ourselves with knowledge of the prize at the end of our wait. Still, waiting is commendable and patience is a virtue. We will certainly dive into the truth of that statement later, but for now, just know this: The city chick who has been known to drive her wheelchair at full speed to get to her destination quickly is the same one who has grown to learn the unmatched value in exercising her patience on this journey of life.

•••

As I look around, I see so many people in a rush to achieve greatness. They're so focused on the reward, they become hasty, jittery, and anxious, and eventually become ungrateful. In their hastiness, they produced a half-baked idea, only to turn around and wonder why they never reached the level of success they aspired to. Excelling at life takes dedication, excellence, and persistence. All of these attributes are exponentially and undoubtedly maximized when paired with patience.

You may be wondering, *Are there legitimate ways to reach success ridiculously fast?* Sure! In fact, we see overnight successes, or what are perceived to be such, happening all around us. Where? Well, let's consider Internet stars and YouTube celebrities. Even videos going viral can place individuals at high levels of fame. Through the advancement of technology, social media has made fame and notoriety incredibly accessible to so many people.

Are you a naturally funny person? Great! Make a few videos exhibiting your natural talent and personality, and you have a shot at capturing a broad audience. Are you gifted artistically? Create a Facebook business page and an Etsy store to sell your merchandise and grow a customer base.

Is it really that easy? In certain respects, yes. There's no doubt that technology has transformed the timeline in which people accomplish their goals. With a computer and access to the web, you can do anything from setting up your business to purchasing a soil sample on Amazon that was collected from a UFO crash site. No kidding. With a click of a button, the internet becomes a current in which flows almost anything one wants to acquire. But while the internet is definitely a tool that, if used correctly, can be advantageous, it certainly isn't a substitute for hard work.

Every substantial, highly rewarding achievement can be killed by one's inability to operate while maintaining a state of patience.

Patience makes way for excellence. But in today's society, this is not what people want to hear.

Instead, many are enticed to travel the road that is less turbulent. For me, I was blessed early on in life with rocky-road experiences in many areas.

Today, I look back with gratitude, and an appreciation for even the small lessons that have had huge impacts on my mindset. The lesson of the value of patience is one I will never forget. Somehow, in such an undesirable experience, I learned that patience is the secret ingredient to having my cake and eating it too.

• • •

My early days as a middle schooler represent a time in my life when I thought money grew on trees and was a resource that was easy to come by. It's funny that I would think that, as my family was far from rich. Mom worked tirelessly to ensure we had basic necessities. She worked third shift at a nursing home to provide a roof over our heads, clothing, and food.

Time goes by fast as a kid, and although I witnessed mom going back to school, obtaining her degree, and working late hours, I didn't account for the huge sacrifice of time she made to make enough money to keep us afloat.

My naiveté surrounding money changed when I was faced with a learning experience that taught me the correlation between sacrifice, money management, and patience. My lesson came the moment I realized my parents weren't going to cater to my request for name brand clothing.

Allow me to paint this picture for you. Elementary school had very little to do with repping the hottest brands and everything to do with the innocence of being a kid, making friends, and being on your best behavior in order to earn the end-of-quarter pizza party.

But sixth grade was just around the corner, and I knew from watching my oldest sister that middle school would be a totally different animal. The pressures from such a transition were felt from many outlets. Back to school advertisements, television shows, and even fifth grade teachers were all pumping our heads up to get us ready for the next step in the educational system.

Once we graduated from elementary school, we were thrown into a different world of crowded hallways, lockers, greater assignments, and a shift in hormones. I landed in middle school and all of a sudden started caring more about what I looked like and how my hair was styled. I no longer wanted to wear the discount kids' clothes my mom picked out for me at J.C. Penney.

Mom had a pretty good deal, being able to fit her preteen daughter into toddler clothing. It worked for me, too, in prior years. But in middle school, I made up my mind that I no longer wanted to wear cute little outfits decorated with strawberries and unicorns.

The summer prior to the start of 6th grade, my style had upgraded to that of my favorite urban music artists from the 90s. Blue jeans, a silver figaro necklace, permed hair, ultra-shiny lip gloss, and a reputable name brand plastered across my chest comprised the look I admired and aimed for. In my community, being a major player in the social arena depended on several ironic contradicting factors. I watched as fellow students boasted about being unique and standing out from the crowd, yet they conformed to popular trends just to be considered stylish. I recognized the social game immediately. It was a risky game to subscribe to, but in my excitement to belong, I brushed off my concerns and followed my classmates into the trap.

Name brand clothing was expensive, but the trap contained some irresistible bait. Wearing a certain logo or name on our apparel somehow gained us popularity points and conveyed that we could afford the finer things. In all actuality, *we* couldn't afford anything. It was our parents who were shelling out the funds.

My humor and wittiness won me popularity in elementary school; all I needed now was the attire to match. Scoping out a few brands that made clothing in my size, I made a list of the items I wanted and the places I could get them.

With only a few months left of summer break, I confidently made my request known to my mother. Definitely an unwise decision on my part. She informed me that her pockets were not going to accommodate my materialistic wants.

The truth was, my parents could care less about fitting in. Fit in? According to my mother, I had better "fit in" those books! Hardheaded and strong-willed, I left my pitching session with my mom both disappointed, and convinced she knew nothing about being cool. But I was determined to get what I wanted. If my mom wasn't going to help me, then I would have fund my longing to fit in myself.

The first step in my plan was to figure out ways to acquire enough money to keep my dressers full of department store threads rather than thrifty ones. With back-to-school shopping rapidly approaching, I knew I had to earn money quickly. I already had a jumpstart, being wise enough to save my birthday money, which I'd neatly and secretly folded under my bunkbed.

But with the steep price of some of my desired items, along with the added cost of school supplies, I needed to come up with more cash. So I got my sister onboard and we began finding chores around the house (the ones I was already assigned didn't count) and scouring the living room furniture for loose change.

My parents also allowed us to earn a few extra bucks playing "restaurant" with them. I would come up with a list of snacks we could prepare for them and my sister and I would serve our creations. A dollar for peanut butter and jelly sandwich, twenty-five cents for one glass of water, and fifty cents for a cup of juice. Earning about five dollars every two days and having to split our revenue in half turned me into a penny pincher for sure. At the end of each week, I'd go to my room, shut my door, and grab my wallet from my secret hiding spot under my bed. My heart would be pounding as I ripped open my Velcro wallet and began counting the dollar bills and change.

At the end of every tally, I remember thinking that there was no way I could save enough money to buy everything I wanted before school started. The amount I saved paled in comparison to the cost of a brand new Nike jacket or FUBU outfit I wanted so badly.

Battling disappointment, all I could think was, *It's going to take forever to earn the money I need doing all these cheesy chores. Why can't my mom and dad be like all the other parents who buy their kids whatever they want?* All the kids in the neighborhood bragged nonstop about their name brand clothing and the popular kicks on their feet. I wanted that—to be like them—more than anything.

Immersed in my frustration, I didn't realize that life was teaching me a valuable lesson not only about discipline, but also about understanding that not every desire comes easily. I was also learning the sobering fact that not everything I wanted was meant for me to have.

There will be times in our lives where a roadblock, such as a lack of resources, will cause our timeline for success to be extended. How many of us have thought, *If I had more money, more assets, if I was just connected to the right person, I'd get where I wanted to be faster?* This may be true in some situations, but my experience in middle school instilled in me a different frame of mind. Instead of wanting *more* to get *more*, consider using what you already have. Use your personal strengths and current resources wisely and endure the process.

My shortsightedness as a preteen taught me a rich lesson that has stayed relevant throughout my life. I ended up shopping for school with a totally different outlook than I expected. Although disappointed at the sluggish increase of my net worth, I now thought twice about the clothes being rung up at the store. Did I really need them? Were they *worth* the money? Suffice to say, I had a new appreciation for the struggle to get to where I wanted to be, and the time and dedication required. Alternately, I learned that the struggle doesn't have to be deemed a "struggle" if you appreciated every little step of progress.

Like learning to ride a wild horse, life's lessons often require falls and bruises along the way. Many of the lessons we learn as children are bricks with which we build our foundation. Although we don't always pay that much attention, these lessons give us a blueprint of how to handle similar situations in the future. However, just because we learn a principal and are comfortable applying it in a certain area of our lives, it's not uncommon to have difficulty applying it in other areas.

The importance of saving and managing money was just one chapter in my personal book of learning patience. Little did I know, there were more chapters and different scenarios to come.

Choosing to Lose

Most people want to be seen as hardworking. But when it comes to backing it up with your actions, it can be easy to search out alternative ways of getting things done. Ways that require less time, energy and resources. Because again, wanting to take the easy way out is a common impulse. An impulse I even found myself having after setting a goal to lose ten pounds. At two feet tall, losing ten pounds is a huge endeavor for me. But I am no different than most people, and losing weight can be a challenge for anyone. It's not a secret, how difficult weight loss can be. According to research, fifty percent of Americans are either trying to lose weight or maintain their current weight. So what does that mean? It means there's a high likelihood that you have or will be faced with the challenge of shedding pounds.

The first time I decided to lose weight, I was pumped. It was a new and exciting challenge, but one that I also underestimated big time. Starting off, I became fascinated with health stores such as GNC and DICK'S Sporting Goods. Even the minimal workout clothes at my local department store were appealing. Neon, pink, blue, and green. Shirts, leggings, and tank tops. If one could look this good while getting in shape, how difficult could be?

My next step was changing my diet. Fruit smoothies here, grilled chicken there. All of it sounded great to me. I was so sure I had everything I needed in hand, but I had no idea how to actually lose weight. There were just too many options and methods. That's when it hit me—this wasn't going to be as quick or easy as I'd thought.

With so many different claims, programs, and choices, I had to do research to find the best way for me to "choose to lose." After collecting data, I found a stark difference in the weight loss methods available. I called them Method A and Method B. Method A represented the more traditional way of losing weight; it's worked for ages, but also requires more effort and discipline.

Working out diligently, eating healthy, and changing bad habits were all that was required to take up Method A. Method B, on the other hand, encompassed all the nontraditional ways of trimming fat. Among the quick fixes advertised were taking a certain pill, drinking a certain shake, and wearing a special garment. Many swore by these various techniques, most of which were known for their convenience and promise of fast results. After looking at all that was presented to me, I found that if used safely, either method would provide results, but there was one that was best for me. My choice wasn't based on the length of time required to reach my goal. Eating healthy and exercising was simply the route that felt right.

Initially, I stood firm in my decision. Yet with every passing day, the compulsion to jump ship and find a new method grew. Nevertheless, I found encouragement and strength in succeeding slowly but steadily. So what were the takeaways from my road to weight loss? First, I realized that many people were actively facing the same decision I was. Struggling to lose weight? Don't worry, you're in good company. You can do it.

Secondly, my experience became about more than losing weight. I felt pressured to settle for one of those popular, alternative methods. Whether I chose Method A or Method B, it was important for me to make my choice based on the results I needed and how I needed them, regardless of the amount of time it would take.

How many poor decisions we have made that ended up sending us down paths that weren't suitable for us in the first place? And how many of those decisions have rested upon our inability to be vigilant and patient?

• • •

Now you may be wondering, *Monique, why is it so bad to want to achieve great things in a short amount of time?* Now, on the surface, I actually don't think it's a bad thing at all. Sometimes we are blessed with the opportunity to leap over stepping stones, or discover helpful shortcuts that help us reach our destination faster.

However, one major caveat is that you must know when and how to use shortcuts. It's easy to get so excited at the first sign of a shortcut that we apply it to the wrong situation. This pitfall can affect some of the most important and sensitive areas of our lives. We take shortcuts in relationships, occupations, management of finances, and more. For example, I knew of a guy who shared with me how his previous hustle to sell knockoff electronics for quick cash almost cost him the life of clean living he leads now. If you're not careful, a shortcut can lead to a dead end, forcing you to begin the process all over again.

Achieving success at an accelerated rate can also be a hindrance to progress. For this reason, much of my decision making begins with the old adage, *Is it too good to be true?* Considering this question has more often than not prevented me from taking dangerous risks and has helped avoid the following three pitfalls.

Developing Unrealistic Expectations

Have you ever met someone who seems to be riding a lucky wave? A wave that keeps them at the height of success without ever bringing them down? And you wonder how that can be? You know that everyone experiences hardships at some point or another. It's an inevitable facet of life. But this individual seems to be living with a genie in a bottle. With a couple of rubs to the bottle, *poof,* their genie appears and offers to grant unlimited wishes. So you scratch your head wondering what you're doing wrong, and why you have to endure so many challenges.

The road to success can be so slow that you find yourself preoccupied with another's fast paced development. The grass is greener on the other side, right? Wrong. The race is not given to the swiftest, but to the one who continues to progress with faith and endurance. The race is given to the one who is able to learn from their mistakes and extract the right principles. The value of enduring challenges lies in developing the right temperament needed to enjoy a potentially long, arduous journey to success.

Having an easy road can stifle your personal growth and development. People who frequently look for the easy way out can also be sidetracked by a "get rich quick" mindset, which ultimately distorts their expectations of life.

As a society, we're so advanced and developed that we've become blind to the fact that tried-and-true success often comes with a bit of resistance. And it should. The road less traveled will help you mentally prepare for when the tide throws you off your lucky wave and sends you crashing into the water. Your mental strength ought to grow big enough to sustain you when you feel like giving up. But the expectation that success will come on your time, without sacrifices and patience, can cripple your ability to overcome challenges in life.

The good news is that everyone is capable of rerouting their thinking back to looking at life with a sound mind. A sound mind does not mean you don't make way for the extraordinary miracles and blessings that will propel you toward your destiny.

Having realistic expectations doesn't mean that you damper, downgrade, or limit your aspirations to only what you see. In fact, your level of motivation should increase as your dreams remain as vibrant, wild, and enormous as ever. But by relinquishing your dependence on unrealistic expectations, you can learn to respect the process, and appreciate the blessings and miracles that grace your journey with delight.

Respecting the process means you are willing to endure setbacks and even failures if the experience opens your horizons and prepares you for the fruits of your labor.

If we are used to getting quick results all the time, we will be disappointed when we come to a task that demands more of us. A task that makes you feel like you're swimming against the current. It may be uncomfortable to endure the challenge, but life isn't always fair. Things won't always pan out the way you hope. The sooner you're able to come to grips with this, the sooner you'll be able to apply effort where it's best suited for the success you aim to achieve.

Experience Unreliable Success

Some of the wealthiest and healthiest individuals I know also enjoy longevity in their success. That's right. I'm not talking about one hit wonders; you know, the ones who are here today and gone tomorrow. I'm talking about people who have chosen to distribute their talents in such a way that they're not concerned with the amount of time it takes to achieve success. Instead of rushing to the finish line, they take strategic steps in the right direction. They fix their eyes on what comes after the race. Those who focus on the greater picture aren't easily distracted by the swift progression of others around them. They stay their course, confident as to where they're headed.

This is seldom the case for those who desire to reach greatness expeditiously. One of the easiest ways to find yourself suffering from a downturn of fortune is to underestimate the power of a strong foundation. People who don't exercise patience build their foundation with inexpensive, flaky materials to get quick results. My advice? *Don't do it.* There's nothing more disheartening than achieving success, then having it stripped away because you didn't know how to maintain it. And get this: Success is only hard to maintain if you don't have the right tools.

The whole point of taking time to build your base is to develop your skills with less chaos and a firm outlook. The secret to longevity is simple. Take one step at a time. During each step, make sure you're learning and developing the work ethic needed to reach the next step. This is the natural way of things. The way success is groomed and conditioned.

Consider the natural progression of a child in school. They start off in a grade level conducive to their intellect and abilities. As children learn, develop, and grow, they are progressively given greater, more challenging tasks. By the time they reach junior high, they are capable of so much more than when they first started school. At this point, children are given more privileges, which come with more responsibilities. Greater privileges, greater responsibilities. The same rings true for everything we strive to accomplish.

Don't skip ahead of the process; it may cost you your dreams.

Lack of Experience

Taking the fast and cheap way to success also places you in a compromising position on the vast, competitive playing field. There's little more detrimental to your goals than growing too fast, experiencing struggle and failure, but not being able to learn from your mistakes.

Know this—No matter which area of success you're aiming to thrive in, there will always be competition. There will always be someone trying to make a bigger impact, working just as hard or even harder to out-run and out-last you.

Imagine arriving at your destination, only to be surpassed by someone who has learned and honed skills you don't possess. Imagine being denied access to your full potential because you didn't take the time to develop the wisdom required to obtain such a high level of success. News flash! It happens all the time.

Don't be convinced that the long road to success is futile. When you find yourself having that thought, dismiss it. If others are implying that it's pointless, disregard their advice. The reality is that the long road equips you with invaluable experiences.

Just recently, I saw a meme on social media that poked fun at the difficulty of finding a job right out of college. The image portrayed and the caption were humorous, but also telling of the importance of experience. Graduates were not being hired because they did not have experience.

**Experience makes you more
trustworthy, confident, and qualified.**

It's no wonder nearly every occupation requires experience. Employers want workers who have operated in their field because they are more likely to possess the skills needed to represent the company well. The same holds true in life.

Time spent allows for the gaining of experience. Time and experience create a fertile ground for developing wisdom and insight.

**Experience begets deeper knowledge and an understanding
that quick success cannot render.**

Bottom line, people respect you more when you can say that your journey wasn't rushed. You have more to offer the world when you have a testimony of where you've been.

How to Tackle Being Impatient

Rushing to succeed is not wise. But now what? How do you fight the urge to move quickly down the road to success? The desire for instant gratification can be very tough to overcome. It can be done by exercising your willpower to focus on your progression.

The first step is making sure you have a plan in place. Without a plan, you have no way of charting your course or measuring your results. Without a plan, you will experience inconsistency, and are more likely to wander aimlessly through life. Trust me, there is nothing more confusing or frustrating than traveling without a map.

Take a moment to think about the following questions. *What does success look like for you?* You may have one overarching definition, but consider smaller successes as well. *What do those mean to you?* Group all your goals together. Write them down. Look at them. Internalize them. Then separate them into two categories: long-term and short-term goals.

Now, hopefully my mention of short-term and long-term goals hasn't sent your eyes rolling in annoyance. Many people have been taught how to set goals, as well as how important it is to distinguish between short-term and long-term. However, in teaching this material every year, I'm continually amazed by how many people know how to set goals, but never implement this knowledge. If this describes you, or if you've never learned about short-term and long-term goals, fret not. Perhaps this is the nudge you need to get started. Let's jump in by examining the process I take to sustain success in my life.

• • •

I begin by writing a list of goals I'm setting out to achieve. Then, I separate them into short-term and long-term. For me, short-term goals are those I strive to conquer within six months or less. For instance, if I have checked off everything on my daily to-do list, that's one goal achieved. If I have set out to finish a painting within two months, and get it done within that timeframe, that is also a goal achieved.

On the other hand, there are goals that fall into the long-term category. These are usually larger, more strenuous goals that require a greater amount of time than six months. Achieving long-term goals tends to parallel major steppingstones in my life. They are the milestones that yield a great outcome, and the accomplishments I find myself proudest of.

An example is when I entered law school in 2009. My long-term goal was to roll across the stage at graduation and obtain my law degree. This was a feat I focused on for three years, and my diligence on even the toughest of days brought me to *the* moment. I crossed the stage, was hooded by my dean, and viewed my family in the crowd cheering me on.

Writing down my goals helps direct the application of my determination. The accomplishment of one goal gives me the motivation and confidence to set the next one.

LET'S SOAR!

Jotting down goals is a beginning step to spreading our wings to fly. Let's take a moment to focus on yours.

SHORT-TERM GOALS: What are a few goals you would like to complete in six months or less? Jot them down here.

_____

_____

_____

_____

_____

LONG-TERM GOALS: Write down a few goals you know will take you in excess of six months to complete.

_____

_____

_____

_____

_____

Take a look at your list. Now take a look at those goals that will require a great amount of time and hard work to come to fruition. Think about how happy you will be when you have achieved those goals. After you've considered these details, know that in the midst of fulfilling your long-term goals, working hard, and even struggling to stay on course, shortcuts will entice you.

Shortcuts will test your true level of patience. Shortcuts will try to convince you that the easier, cheaper route is better than what looks like a long and agonizing road to success. Don't spend so much time admiring the outcome of the long-term goal that you overlook the appropriate time it takes to reach that goal.

Impatience opens the door for cheating, greed, ungratefulness, laziness, and settling for less. Don't forfeit the benefits of the process for the sake of potentially disastrous shortcuts. And when you are feeling tempted to ditch the high road for the low, remember this: *To forsake is a mistake.*

The Takeaway

You are the only one who can determine what success means in your life. No one can make you feel like a success or failure but you.

Are these statements true? Of course they are. But they are hard concepts to internalize because we're constantly being fed society's definition of success. You are the only one who, at the end of your life, can determine whether or not you're satisfied with your actions and accomplishments.

Therefore, you must set the standards in your life. When I made a conscious decision to live with the right standards, I became free. Free to operate under the purpose for which I was created. This freedom will have its own meaning and impact in your life. Personally, I found that it enhanced my faith, my walk with God, and helped me realize that my potential could not be stifled by anyone but me.

The possibilities and opportunities in life are limitless. This is true for you, too. When and from where they come, we won't always know. Seek the type of success that grows when nurtured and yields a good harvest. Patience is not only a virtue, but the key to unlocking your dreams.

LETS SOAR!

Can you identify some past experiences in which you made hasty decisions? What kind of adjustments can you make today to increase your level of patience?

_____

_____

_____

_____

_____

_____

_____

_____

_____

_____

_____

_____

_____

_____

LESSON FOUR

Naysayers

"

NEVER ALLOW NAYSAYERS TO PULL YOU OFF TRACK!

🐦 @madetwosoar

"

Hindsight is 20/20, and that experience of my final IEP meeting proved to be a gold mine of lessons for me. That's why, today, I can motivate people to get excited about their futures, even when they have little support. No matter how frustrated they are, I confidently tell them, "Forget the junk spewed at you."

What people say about you today doesn't have to rule your future.

Your best defense is to be prepared. Know what's coming at you and how you'll deal with it. Sooner or later, you'll meet the antagonists of your life's story. You know, the ones who will oppose you and try to stand in the way of your success. They can be the most difficult individuals to accept as part of your process. But they're necessary.

Coming to grips with accepting the role of naysayers in your life is difficult, especially when you're in the heat of opposition and facing potential rejection. But know this: You own the power to take the feedback of your naysayers and make it beneficial to you. Accepting the presence of naysayers doesn't mean you have to agree with their judgements about you. Instead, it's about reversing their pessimistic views into tools that hone your success. Sound like an impossible feat? Nothing is impossible.

Before we dig into how to confront naysayers, let me throw a curve ball and ask, *Who do you consider to be a naysayer?* One of the trending topics today, especially with our youth, is having "haters." The term "hater" has been popularized by my generation, and is synonymous with naysayer.

And as with many terms, when used excessively its meaning becomes diluted. The term "hater" has certainly fallen into this category. Perhaps that's the reason I haven't embraced the "I have haters" trend. It diverts my attention away from what really matters. Just because someone disagrees with me and I subsequently label them as a hater, doesn't actually mean they feel hatred toward me. Such an insinuation counteracts one's ability to live happily. And yet, I know that many people struggle with adversity.

When I speak on naysayers, my aim is not to cast aspersions on individuals who may not see things totally your way. If we're not careful, our ego can distort the truth. Be wary of the "I have haters" mentality, as it can define you as a stubborn, know-it-all.

Know the Difference

Know the difference between a naysayer and someone with merely an opposing thought. What is a naysayer? The label carries around a negative connotation of someone who works against you in meaningful aspects of your life. So be careful to whom you assign the title.

Know the difference between a naysayer who is simply trying to rain on your parade, and a person whose thoughtful insight might contradict your ideas. Knowing the difference allows you to respond responsibly after processing the feedback in an unbiased manner.

One of the most common mistakes people make while defending their dreams is disregarding valuable information because the person delivering it has differing opinions. Just because someone doesn't see your dreams the way you do, doesn't mean their feedback isn't worth considering. Approach it like this:

Be bold and confident enough to dance to the beat of your own drum, but keep an ear out for the beats of others.

Give yourself the opportunity to learn from someone else. In doing so, you gain understanding and equip yourself with what's needed to perfect, adjust, and rightly defend your dreams. When your aspirations are on trial, the stage is set for you to show others what you're capable of.

• • •

Speaking of stages, a great example of this involves one of my favorite shows on primetime television, *Shark Tank*. From the very first time I watched an episode of the show, I was hooked. I found myself searching for and tuning in to every episode of every season. Every Friday, I carved out time in my schedule to gather the family and watch the new episode as it aired.

Captivated, I even became an avid viewer of the show's Canadian version, *Dragons' Den*. Talk about a fan! What made me so attracted to the show? Well, if you're not familiar, allow me to explain its premise. Each episode features a group of four or five motivated entrepreneurs who pitch their business ideas to wealthy investors, known as the Sharks (or Dragons on *Dragons' Den*).

Elements of the show are quite conservative and structured. However, the producers do an outstanding job of keeping viewers on edge by featuring unique entrepreneurs with creative, useful, and sometimes bizarre ideas. Besides being highly entertaining, there are other reasons I stayed up some nights (often past midnight) to binge watch previous seasons.

First, the show directly connects with my core identity of entrepreneur, artist, and creator. I'm inspired by watching people from all walks of life boldly and passionately share their ventures on national television. A huge leap of faith is required to take such a risk, and attests to the fact that drive, passion, and hard work are accessible to people of all ethnicities, locations, and cultures.

Another key feature of *Shark Tank* is the persuasive manner with which each entrepreneur delivers their presentation. Not everyone who comes on the show is overly confident. I've seen some presenters whose body language screamed fear and intimidation as they tripped over words or forgot part of their pitching script. Despite their clear struggle, they were still on national television determined to reach their goal. And after their initial pitch, it was always exciting to see whether they could strike a deal with an investor.

The investors have to be willing to invest the amount of money the entrepreneurs are asking for. The sharks operate on financial principles. They remain strictly disciplined, sometimes willing to take risks, but overall aiming to remain good stewards of their money. Great show, right? But aside from the business pointers one could glean from watching, there's also a valuable lesson that can be learned about rejection. Not every pitch has a fairytale ending. In fact, many don't.

The investors are called Sharks for a reason. When Sharks disagree with an entrepreneur, or think the pitch is a poor one, they have absolutely no qualms about expressing disapproval. Due to the time limits of the show, Sharks don't bother sugar-coating their responses. Often, their feedback is blunt and borderline offensive. Contestants have become angry, argumentative, and some have left with tears in their eyes.

Rejection of your dreams with an audience of millions is sure to produce raw emotion. So how *should* someone respond to such blunt criticism from successful, self-made investors? Some of the invited entrepreneurs totally disregard the feedback, while others decide to learn from the experience. This willingness to consider the comments from the Sharks is due to the inherent value of the Sharks' entrepreneurial successes.

Have the Sharks been wrong? Of course. But I've learned that although your naysayers aren't always right, some of their thoughts are worth considering, as they might shed light on how to improve your game plan.

Take a commentator or naysayer's opinion (the ones worth listening to), extract the good, throw out the bad, and never look back.

Do We Need the Advice of Others?

"Ugh, Monique, it looks fine to me," said my sister, Tanya, after I summoned her to the living room to take yet another look at my painting. It was the one-hundred and fourteenth time she'd answered my call, and been gracious enough to come take a peek. Her graciousness had finally worn thin.

"You don't have to have an attitude... but thanks," I mumbled as she walked away.

Although she was supportive from afar, art wasn't my sister's passion. There was nothing I could do about that. Believe me, I tried everything, including probing her to answer questions about my methods, asking her to stare at the painting, and even offering her a dollar to give genuine feedback.

The first couple of times I tried them, these methods worked, but nothing would ever cure her disinterest. After a while, I started questioning why I even continued to ask her. Sometimes, I felt that I was wasting my time. And deep down I knew I was being annoying. I repeatedly told myself, *Monique, be independent. Think for yourself. Make autonomous decisions. You're an artist!* But the desire for my older sister's approval remained. So for as long as she'd make the twelve-step journey from the dining room, I kept calling.

Why do we seek validation from others? Is it a healthy practice? In some respects, it is. In completing a work assignment, you may seek the advice of a coworker or supervisor. Before publishing this book, I sought feedback from editors, writers, and formatters. For the content, I even sought the advice of those within my target audience. I had a lot of knowledge, but there was still a lot to learn. In an attempt to better myself, I put my ideas out there. Some feedback was difficult to identify with, and some I opted not to adopt.

Anytime you share your dreams with another, be prepared for the possibility of resistance. Speaking from experience, it doesn't feel good to have others disagree with your goals. But while enduring resistance is tough, when processed correctly, it will make you stronger.

LET'S SOAR!

Who are the individuals you trust? From whom do you seek feedback most often? Try to name five people who fit in this category.

_____

_____

_____

_____

_____

_____

Which of their characteristics prompt you to value their opinions?

_____

_____

_____

_____

_____

_____

Have you ever woken up with a crazy idea that's both brilliant and a bit scary? An idea that you know was given to you for a reason, but you don't know how others will receive it? Or how about this: Have you ever shared your aspirations with someone, and afterwards realized that you were the only one truly excited about them? I'm certain it has happened to you, and if not, get ready.

The journey to success requires a healthy level of autonomy. You're headlining, so you'd better show up to your own show. But as we explored in chapter two, we are social beings who benefit from interacting with others. Everyone, in some respect, values the feedback and input of others. Special reverence is often placed on the opinions of those we care for and who hold a respected role in our social circles. It is a natural delight to have the support and encouragement of others. But here comes an important newsflash...

Not all of our ideas will receive the validation and support we want. At some point, we will all face the opposition of others in the form of opinions and advice. Some of these incidents you will be able to handle with ease. Others, not so much. But if you don't know how to handle the naysayers in your life, you may jeopardize the fruition of your dreams, or misjudge the situation and ruin good relationships. Either outcome works against you living your best life.

Successful people invest in their own happiness, experiencing the best opportunities, goals, and relationships. And because they focus on the joys of life, they aren't afraid to share their life and ideas with others, even if there's a chance of criticism. Their minds are free of adversaries, and their lives are free of people who plant seeds of doubt. They understand that living successfully means not allowing naysayers to inhibit their process and progress.

Ask yourself how you react to people who have little faith in you and your abilities. How do you deal with individuals who are not in agreement with you? How do you handle your naysayers?

To answer these questions, begin with a healthy state of mind. You should start off by acknowledging that everyone is different. Each individual has his or her own unique make up, complete with personal ideas, interests, and capabilities. Likewise, every person possesses a distinct outlook on life, and is guided by his or her own moral compass.

The collection of our unique points of view is what keeps this world spinning with creativity. Every person is entitled to an opinion, and should be free to voice it. When you truly accept this, it will ease your mind and guard your heart. Maintaining perspective will keep you from being easily unsettled by what others say. Why? Because you know that no one is going to think exactly like you do, and that's totally fine.

Killing your dreams because of someone else's opinions is simply not worth it.

Enjoying the road to success requires exercising wisdom in order to avoid conflicts and unnecessary robbery of your happiness.

• • •

Wisdom and discernment are two of the most important qualities you can have, especially when dealing with people. Wisdom is affordable to everyone, but requires maturity and a level head. Our dreams and ideas are precious to us. So it's no wonder we become emotionally invested in them. There is nothing wrong with this, but our emotions can muddy our thoughts and affect our productivity. It is possible to become so emotionally invested that we are crushed when we meet an adversary. Negative feedback can cause us to be so entangled in the views of others that we lose sight of our goals.

I have witnessed the demise of individuals whose unhealthy response to criticism paralyzed their success.

We can be so angry, saddened, and shocked by criticism that we become counterproductive. Our focus shifts from a place of optimism and inspiration to a place of doubt and frustration. Our time and energy is wasted on negativity. An ordinary person wallows in this feeling, but an extraordinary individual does the opposite, processing the response of naysayers in a way that fosters personal growth. With the right mindset, the words of your adversary can add to your ultimate wellbeing. But it takes maturity and understanding.

As you can imagine, I've experienced opposition in countless ways. My perspective on naysayers has developed over the years to a point where I'm able to easily identify the source, the energy behind the source, and whether their opinion is relevant and beneficial to me.

Naysayers Identified

Your skeptics will come in all shapes and sizes and have various connections to you. There is no association too distant or too close to exclude the possibility of a person being a naysayer. It can be a total stranger or your best friend. Be prepared and ready to handle them when they come.

When you find yourself receiving negativity from another, consider the source. Account for a person's reputation, background, and knowledge, along with their relation to you. It may seem like a lot to consider, but trust me, it's important. Ask yourself why you even consider their point of view to be in conflict with yours. Is it what they said? How they acted? Then think about what this person means to you. How much value do you place on their input?

Typically, the more valuable you consider a person to be, the higher the likelihood that their perspective will impact you and your decision making. The depth of a relationship with a person guides how we respond to their behavior. If you like the person or have invested emotionally with them, you may be more willing to listen and consider their point of view. It's simply a game of understanding yourself in relation to others, and being mindful of personal behaviors you want to change.

Source's Energy

Never take what others say as mere words. Just as actions have consequences, words spoken have meaning. They all come from of a place of positivity or negativity.

When receiving feedback from others, identify the energy behind it.

Ask yourself why a person feels the way they do. That three letter word—WHY—opens the door to a lot of information. When someone is judging your dreams, ask for an explanation of their thoughts. An explanation will help you decide the validity of their point of view, while also giving you a peek at their true intentions.

Acting on their own person fears, the biggest naysayers in my life have used words to try steering me in directions counter to my dreams.

The people who try to deter you from living your dreams either lack faith, or aren't living their own dreams.

One way to tell if a person is guided by fear is to determine whether they confine themselves, are risk-averse, or have never broken past impossible-seeming barriers.

Only fear—fear of failing, fear of risk, fear of standing out—will keep a person stuck to the ground instead of soaring with opportunities. Being fearless doesn't mean you act recklessly or foolishly. And because I'm naturally a more risk-adverse person, this took me a while to understand. When it came to making some important decisions in my life, my naysayers' comments were imprinted in my thoughts. For a time, their words were at war with my God-given ideas and abilities.

Before long, I found myself immobilized by external forces that truly meant me no good. In my state of paralysis, I also took on my naysayers' worry, agony, and fear. It took boldness to question my adversaries' positions. It took being fed up for me to realize that others' fear was affecting my happiness. Being fearful is miserable, and misery loves company. So always be on alert for signs that fear is at the root of the feedback you're receiving.

• • •

Jealousy can also poison naysayers' opinions about your aspirations. I've wrestled with this truth in my own personal life for two reasons. First, I truly believe that everyone has light within them. Depending on the life they lead, some lights shine bright, while others flicker, barely able to stay on. Because I look for the good in everyone, jealousy is not the first thing that comes to mind when I engage with potential naysayers. Secondly, I often wonder how anyone could be jealous of me. Who would want to deter me (little old me) from my path to success? Surely I don't have anything that others would want? But these thoughts were far from the truth.

A person's jealousy is not always based on superficial attributes like looks. They might covet your happiness, talents, and well being. You may not think you pose a threat to anyone, but true happiness is easily recognizable in your attitude and behavior. When you are happy, productive, and unstoppable, you become highly attractive to others. Happiness is magnetic, and pulls both good and not-so-good. While you can't always control who walks into your life and what they say, you can control how you respond. You can choose whether or not you allow them to affect you.

When others don't work as hard as you, and yet want what you have, they might fall prey to jealousy. Operating from this negative mindset, they can throw you off your game by making you doubt what you're doing, where you're going, and what you're capable of achieving. Don't let them get the best of you. In fact, don't let a naysayer get *anything* from you besides more drive and dedication to your dreams.

Combating Self-Doubt

"EMBRACE CONFIDENCE BOLDLY.

@madetwosoar

Honestly, when my mother shared with me that a world of possibilities would be at my fingertips if I worked hard and believed, I don't think she expected such a clichéd phrase to impact me so much. Or maybe she did. But there's a good chance she doesn't even remember speaking those words into my little ears and thereby my consciousness.

As I shared earlier, my mother's words have guided me through many challenges. In my heart, mind, and soul, I've done whatever I can to take advantage of life and its opportunities. Therefore, it was second nature to take my mom's inspirational message and integrate it into my belief system. Regardless of whether she remembers her specific words to me, I know she sees them reflected in my actions.

Building up my foundation and self-esteem, telling me that I could do anything, was like giving me the keys to a treasure chest that stored my superwoman cape. I felt invincible and boundless, which probably frightened my parents and assistants. But it was too late—a spark had been ignited. Watch out world, I was going to be rolling in a city near you.

Birthed With Confidence

I laughed hysterically when my friend told me about her son's explorative feats around their beautiful home. Little Caleb, not yet one-year-old, had mastered crawling, pulling up on surfaces, and was on the brink of walking unassisted. I watched him on the go, playing in their living room, which was gated from the kitchen.

"So, how has he gotten along with Lizzy and Titi?" I asked his parents as I beheld Caleb's shining grin. Lizzy and Titi were the family's Chihuahuas.

"They get along for the most part," said Caleb's father. "Lizzy and Titi get a bit jealous of our new bundle of joy, but Caleb isn't afraid of them."

I was glad to hear this, but what his father said next caught me off guard.

"I tell you, we have to watch Caleb. One day we caught him chowing down on a dog treat. We have no idea how he got to it."

Laughing, I looked at Caleb with a newfound amazement. "Was it good?" I asked him, my face scrunched up in distaste.

Caleb's joyful return smile led me to believe that maybe the treat wasn't so terrible, after all. At that moment, I envied him a little. Through his innocence, he was capable of doing what many people aren't able to. That is, living without the fear of being different.

Have you ever had the chance to observe children from infancy to toddlerhood? It is truly one of the most amazing things I've ever witnessed. It's true, babies are sure to bring on a case of cuteness overload. But even deeper than that, watching the progression of their personality and mindset is both mind-boggling and encouraging.

Each day as they develop and grow, they become more inquisitive of their surroundings and are willing to explore fearlessly whatever captivates their minds. For the past year, I've had a chance to observe my new twin nephews. It is an extreme joy to be active and to participate in their daily lives, and to witness innocence and self-confidence in their purest states.

The times we've had to grab a heel of a foot to keep one of them from taking a leap of faith off the bed are too many to count. After the heart palpitations go away and the chill-bumps disintegrate, as grownups we say to ourselves, *What were the little ones thinking?*

Babies don't realize danger until they learn about consequences. Until then, every child acts upon the "can-do" attitude they were born with. They aren't confined by self-imposed boundaries or limitations. Put simply, they exercise faith and self-trust. Although their thinking might be skewed and undeveloped, there is beauty in how intrinsically confident they are.

Infants and toddlers go after their desires wholeheartedly. In fact, they are relentless, and will ignore our discipline to achieve what they want. Becoming a new auntie has made me fully aware of this. A baby's determination certainly keeps their caregivers on their toes, and the childproofing industry growing steadily. How very little infants are afraid of is incredible, as is their willingness to try almost anything presented to them. They live and engage with the world without the weight of worry.

The life lessons don't stop when infants move to the next stage of development. Advancing to their toddler and adolescent years, their creativity blossoms. They engage more with others and express themselves more freely. As the child continues to grow, so does their desire to have more freedom and explore new levels of liberation. Having access to life's opportunities becomes even more important than it was before.

As my memory takes me back to childhood, such was certainly true in my life. Just thinking of myself in my younger days puts me into a state of amazement over how innocent and inspired my thinking was. But of course, we all tend to think the grass is greener on the other side.

As a youngster, though I enjoyed all the advantages of being a kid, I also looked forward to adulthood. I marveled at all the possibilities whenever I was asked the familiar question, "What do you want to be when you grow up?"

Certainly not taking into account all the responsibilities that come with adulthood, I craved the autonomy associated with being a grown-up. Grown-ups could drive cars and go wherever they wanted. My parents had the grown-up privilege of setting house rules. And the greatest part of being an adult in my eyes? No bedtimes. *What a blissful life adults lead*, I thought.

But whenever my elders caught wind of us wanting to be grown-ups, they were quick to slow us down. "Pump your breaks, young one, enjoy your childhood. This adult life comes with a lot of responsibility. It's a different world." Their advice was never what I wanted to hear, and did nothing to curb my curiosity and desire to be older. After receiving their unwanted counsel, I invariably felt an even stronger desire to grow up.

When you're a kid, you never think adults understand you. It's as if we believed adults were never children just like us. However, I found that my perception of their advice changed as I grew older.

Middle school served as a prelude to how much consciousness changes as you become exposed to and aware of society. How I viewed the world, my community, my life, and even my existence became more malleable as it was influenced by external forces.

All of a sudden my eyes opened to a reality that my unripe mind didn't know existed. With growing up came a great deal of accountability. I had a responsibility to not only complete educational requirements and household chores, but I also had to maintain my self-identity and defend a healthy perception of my worth.

We were taught as children that sticks and stones may break our bones but words would never hurt us. But as the world became more influential in my life, I found that statement to be untrue. The words spoken to me and about me, the images presented, and the ideals imparted to me were coming from so many different sources that it became increasingly difficult to know truth from lie.

The older I grew, the more my "can-do" attitude shifted from a statement to a question. *Can I do?*

Attuning my senses to society's expectations only clouded my judgment. My thoughts and views were no longer in line with my highest truth.

This headspace can cause you to question yourself, your future, and your abilities. It's a danger zone, enticing you away from your chosen path. It also holds potential to grow into an opposing giant who aims to rob you of your success. One of the most difficult giants to encounter and overcome is self-doubt.

I ran from that giant for a long time. And the more I ran, the more it grew in strength. I soon became tired, but I didn't want to face the truth, so I continued running even though I was exhausted. Finally, the time came when I said, *Enough is enough.* No longer would I allow self-doubt to wreak havoc in my life.

Do you have a giant named self-doubt? We all do. What are you going to do about it? When will you stop running? I can tell you that the moment I stopped running was the moment I regained myself. With this surrender, I was rejuvenated and powerful enough to defeat my giant.

Success was at stake and so was my purpose. My future could not shine brightly with self-doubt over my head, casting its dark shadow.

How do you Defeat Self-Doubt?

In the previous chapter, we learned about naysayers and external forces that can deter us from soaring to great heights. Although addressing these forces brings attention to them, they are only as powerful as we allow them to be.

What gives self-doubt power over you is the power you give it.

Belief dictates our actions and thoughts. We sign up, we subscribe, we support, and we give our energy to what we believe in.

We operate at our best when we know what we believe, and can act in accordance with that belief. Guarding what you believe in your heart is imperative to lasting success. Why? Because your belief system can be easily influenced, and if you're not careful, this can lead to self-inflicted harm.

Part of self-doubt originates in past experiences, specifically the times we've allowed negativity into our consciousness. How do you combat this? Take control over what you hear, see, and think—these main outlets have a profound effect on your ability to defeat self-doubt.

Guard Your Ears

We have a very complex relationship with our ears and their functions. Hearing enhances our quality of life, but it's also a gift many people take for granted. With the ability to hear, we are able to enjoy life's beautiful and harmonious sounds. Sounds that shape every aspect of our lives. Birds chirping at the break of dawn. The rumble of thunder that accompanies bright flashes of lightning in a tumultuous sky. The opening melody at the beginning of your favorite song. Or even the calm, soothing voice of a loved one.

Sounds are all around us. They sit at the base of the words we form in our hearts and minds long before they exit our mouths. While hearing empowers and strengthens us, it also makes us susceptible to external influences.

Unlike speaking, hearing and sight are senses that make us vulnerable to what's happening around us and to us. Hearing what others have to say places us on the receiving end of the communication process. And once a person hears something, it's imprinted in both the conscious and subconscious minds. Nothing that is heard can be unheard. That's what makes spoken words so powerful.

Everyone has been guilty of speaking words into the atmosphere that are unflattering, damaging, and negative. And when these words are spoken to another, they can damage a person's self-esteem and confidence. Just as we must be aware of the words we offer, we must guard what we hear.

Guard Your Eyes

Having the ability to see is much like having the ability to hear. In some instances, what we see can have more of an impact on our lives than what we hear. There is a saying: *seeing is believing*. For many individuals, this is certainly true. Our eyes have the ability to look at an image and process feelings, tastes, and even sounds based on memory and the context of the scene. For example, imagine you're looking at a picture of someone having a steak dinner at an oceanfront restaurant.

Your eyes perceive the glistening shine on the char grilled steak, and your mouth waters as you imagine the taste. Then you lift your gaze, seeing waves crashing on a clear sandy beach. You can almost hear the crash of the water as it meets the shore. The attire of the individuals having dinner indicates that the weather is warm; the water probably is, too.

Just one view of an image can make us totally aware of the scene as if we were there. That's how powerful our eyes can be, and why it is important we don't allow everything to enter into our consciousness through our eyes.

• • •

When I was a kid, I would sit down with my grandfather in front of the television to watch pro-wrestling. Do not ask me why the slamming of bulky, big-muscled dudes in the center of a roaring crowd was entertaining to me, but it was. When a wrestler toted around a shiny championship belt, I was convinced they could beat anyone in the world. There was power and strength being displayed, and I was glued to the television because of it.

I became a fan of wrestling and for a period of about two or three years, each time the fall fair visited my city, I looked forward to playing the game "Guess My Age." It was one of the perks of being a little person. I was sure that the employee working the booth would never guess that I was eight-years-old. Year after year, I was right, and their failure to guess my age correctly gave me the opportunity to pick any prize from their cheesy display. Ignoring the medium to large stuffed animals and cartoon characters, basketballs and footballs toys, I always went directly for the pictures of celebrities.

My chosen prize was either a framed portrait of Tupac (my favorite artist of that day) or, you guessed it, a popular wrestler. Those two pictures hung in my room until I found out the truth behind entertainment based wrestling. My amazement with the televised program came to an abrupt end when I found out from a classmate that the wrestling I tuned into was staged and fake. I felt naïve for having believed in something that was little more than smokescreens and parlor tricks. My belief in wrestling dissipated in front of my eyes. In fact, the only time I ever watched it again was to identify all the bad acting and fake moves. Once you're aware of the truth, it becomes impossible to dismiss it.

One picture can be worth a thousand words, but what we see is not always reality. And sometimes the world around us can paint a picture that affects us in counterproductive ways. The false ideal of beauty, for example, is one image the media continuously tries to sell us. And if we don't know the whole truth, then what we see can become the standard by which we judge ourselves. Another great example would be our interaction with social media. This platform is a wonderful outlet to share our lives with others, let our voices be heard, and to keep up with friends and family. But while social media is a great way to get a sense of someone's life, it does not always tell the whole story. Why? We are more compelled to showcase the flashy, more upbeat aspects of our lives.

If we are not careful, we can perceive an individual through the lens of social media and use it as a standard to measure ourselves. And self-doubt can surface when we feel like we don't measure up.

The visible spectrum is limited, but what we see can influence us greatly. The social media platform represents just one outlet that affects us in this manner. Television, news media, magazines, billboards, music videos, movies, the red carpet at award shows, and many other aspects of society influence how we feel about ourselves. We must guard our eyes and build up an understanding of who we are before allowing our minds to be subjected to another person's suggestions. Guard your eyes.

• • •

There are many ways that negativity can enter our minds. So why would I only highlight eyes and ears? I find that through our eyes and ears is how we receive information that poses the biggest threat to our self-confidence. Unfortunately, we lack a physical shield to protect us from those things we see and hear that threaten our comfort, confidence, and beliefs.

To triumph in this area, we need to counteract the negativity we receive with the truth of who we are. This requires that we first, unashamedly and unapologetically, proclaim our identity. In order to proclaim, we must first understand what we're made of. Recognize all the wonderful characteristics that make you who you are.

Exploring your heritage or lineage is a great way to know where you've come from. It is more than knowing the less desirable attributes of your family. It is knowing your culture and your lineage's contribution to society.

Which tribe, country, or region does your family come from? Did your family immigrate from another land? Or did they overcome a struggle that explains your current location? Perhaps this is your true, native land, and the ground you stand on is land your family owns and cultivates.

Exploring my family's history has been a powerful means of growing my confidence. Knowing that my family includes a unique blend of African, Hispanic, and Native American threads makes me beyond grateful to be the person I am today. And on top of that, the individuals who've contributed to my DNA empower me greatly. In my soul, I know that my ancestors prayed for those who came after them to lead to greater lives than they had. I owe my strength and self-confidence to them.

During moments when I don't feel adequate or intelligent enough, I think of my grandmother, specifically of a black-and-white photo taken before I was born. In the photo, she is dressed in her crisp, white nursing uniform. In spite of the struggles of oppression brought on by society, and in spite of her own personal obstacles, she graduated school and became a nurse. That photo assures me that I am cut from the same cloth of boldness, perseverance, and strength.

You, too, are a new piece of fabric woven from the threads of your ancestor's cloth. Everyone's personal situation is unique. You may feel like your family has failed on too many occasions. You may not even know much about your family's history. But that's okay.

We are all part of the same human family, and if you dig deep enough, you'll find someone whose actions enabled you to exist today. After all, you are here, a blessing from God, because of the actions of your parents, grandparents, and great-grandparents. There is greatness right in your DNA from all your ancestors have overcome and accomplished.

Once you've identified where you come from, define who you are and who you intend to be.

This action can be completed by no one but you. You are the captain of your ship, and where you're going is determined by what you do and how you live. Who are you? Whoever you are, that identity is what you must proclaim and allow your actions to reflect. The clearer you are about who you are, and the more you put it forth into the atmosphere, the sturdier you will be in the fight against self-doubt.

Lastly, I'll share with you my favorite weapon in my arsenal to fight self-doubt. But first, let's understand something. Each and every one of us possesses aspects we would love to have changed. We all have areas of our lives where we've dropped the ball, or felt like we've caused too much damage to be successful. Everyone, no matter how much money they accumulate, their status, upbringing, family history... *everyone* experiences doubt. Knowing this about yourself could easily deter you from striving for success.

My biggest weapon against self-doubt is faith. Instead of dwelling on negative thoughts about myself, I seek help from my Creator. He understands His creations more than anyone else. When I experience moments of doubt, depression, and loneliness, I consult with God. I choose to listen to what He says about me.

Here are a few scripture verses that encourage me:

"Yet in all these things we are more than conquerors through Him who loved us." Romans 8:37

"You are the light of (Christ to) the world. A city set on a hill cannot be hidden." Matthew 5:14

"I praise you, for I am fearfully and wonderfully made. Wonderful are your works; My soul knows it very well."
Psalm 139:14

And the most awesome thing about these statements is that in addition to being true, they apply to you, too. Look into the mirror and proclaim these truths over your life. Speak these positive words to yourself and then don't hold back. Shout them from the mountaintop.

The more you speak positive truth in your life, the more your doubts will lessen.

Doubt will flee from your mind, body, and soul. Stand firm. Know who you are, what you accept, and expect nothing less.

LET'S SOAR!

To counteract self-doubt, remind yourself of your qualifications. Think for a moment of the attributes that make you powerful. What are they?

_____

_____

_____

_____

_____

_____

_____

_____

LESSON SIX

Journeying Alone

" ALONE TIME IS THE BEST TIME TO STUDY YOUR PURPOSE AND MAP OUT YOUR VISION. "

@madetwosoar

Life has a way of teaching you lessons. Lessons that make you reflect on your past experiences and wonder why you didn't learn them sooner. As an adult, I take periodic looks into my past to recall what my outlook on life was at certain times. These reflections aren't to relive past mistakes, which is detrimental to my future state of being. Instead it's more like rereading a page in my journal to see how far I've come.

When I began my entrepreneurial journey, I never expected to be taught a lesson on how to be okay with "riding solo." To help you understand, I'll share a little bit more about me. Anyone who knows me knows that I'm an extrovert. My personality was certainly a gift from God. Considering the attention my physical state garners from the general public, by necessity I've grown comfortable around people. In fact, even in the midst of stares, disrespectful comments, and sometimes being treated as an outcast, I love interacting and surrounding myself with human beings.

Amazingly, I've never let others' treatment of me discount the benefits my social abilities give me. These social abilities have contributed tremendously to the creation of ideas and development of my confidence, and have been an asset that I've utilized throughout my motivational speaking career. I've been surrounded by people my whole life. I grew up in a household with four other siblings, and we each had our circle of friends that intermingled with each other despite our three-year age difference. Even in my everyday life, my daily tasks are typically completed with the assistance of another.

While I wouldn't have classified myself as a wild child in college, I certainly enjoyed every day on campus, surrounded by my friends. My undergraduate career at my alma mater was spent with a great group of friends; we bonded together through everything. For those four years as college students, we helped each other get through difficult classes, relationships, and financial strains. It was an amazing experience with wonderful people.

Although introverts fascinated me, I definitely fell into the same category as the popular kids in high school: loud, spirited, hilarious, and outgoing. I carried those very same traits with me to college. Always down to have a great time. My dorm room was a lively place, with my circle of friends popping in and out all times of the day and night.

My crew of about eight and I were night owls, and often stayed up laughing and socializing until the sun rose. Every year, three of the four suites in my dorm unit were occupied by me and two of my closest friends. Thankfully, we always got along with our forth suite-mate, except for one. She spent her time much differently than we did. Looking back, we likely struck every nerve she had with our extreme amount of socializing. But we just chalked it up to her being antisocial. I'd think to myself, *How can you not enjoy hanging out and being around people?*

I didn't understand her behavior until I posed the question to a friend who described themselves as a loner. Here I was with tons of friends, smiling, greeting, and chatting it up with people everywhere I went. When I considered my friend, I thought they were missing out on a life of fun and excitement. But our dialog taught me a lot. I'd spent a lot of time trying to persuade them to come out of their comfort zone and join me in my party of life. After talking with them a while, however, I began to understand their point of view, and why they preferred sticking to themselves and being an introvert.

Our conversation opened my eyes to a different way of life, and revealed some of the reasons why certain people prefer to keep to themselves. Some people work better alone because they aren't cluttered with opinions that might contradict theirs. Some introverts operate best as observers. They don't feel like they have to speak all the time, be the center of attention, or make themselves known. They would rather sit back and watch, learning from others and growing in wisdom.

On the other hand, there are introverts whose life experience has made them fearful of growing attached to others, primarily because of past disappointments and disloyalty. When I was told this for the first time, it pulled at my heartstrings and made me want to jump into action, to save the day with a pep talk.

My response was always the following: when you are working with people, you have to remember that there will be disagreements and disappointments. We all have different perspectives, opinions, and methods for accomplishing goals, which can cause conflicts.

These conflicts can negatively shape your views on working with others. Some people have been in so many conflicts, and let down so many times, that they refuse to open themselves up to new interactions. I thoroughly believe that this journey of life is not meant for us to endure alone. Collaborating is a wonderful way to fellowship, and to help one another accomplish much in life. I left that conversation feeling like I helped someone.

Not long after, I noticed the emergence of a movement, one that quickly gained popularity and attention among young people. That is, labeling oneself as "self-made." Those who consider themselves self-made focus all of their energy on themselves, and attribute their success to no one else.

This school of thought derives from the desire to be independent, to take control of your life, and to not be reliant on anyone else's contribution. But if we are not careful, we will miss the true essence of working together, which sharpens our skills and knowledge. Having a self-made mentality stunts growth and breeds arrogance. I've always been an advocate of this saying: *Things are better when we do them together.*

For many years, this was a phrase I neither questioned nor deviated from, not knowing that I would later experience disloyalty from friends, and feel disconnected and lonely. Turns out I needed to take my own advice to keep from feeling the hollowness of fear and isolation.

Summer 2012

The summer of 2012 was a roller coaster. The highest point of the ride was graduating from law school. After three long, strenuous years of pouring over case briefs, studying law, and being on edge during every class due to my professor's belief in the Socratic method, it was finally over. Law school was an unforgettable experience that pushed me to limits I never knew existed. It was nothing like I imagined it would be, and my circle of friends certainly didn't grow as wide as I had hoped. But I made it.

With the support of a few of my helpful colleagues, I rolled across the graduation stage with the brightest smile and the most joyful heart. The excitement, however, was short lived. Within a week, I found myself living in a small dorm room, alone and overwhelmed with study material for the North Carolina Bar Exam.

Over the course of two months of studying, my sisters and mother took turns staying with me to assist with personal needs. But with my rigorous schedule, no one could provide the company I needed unless they were studying for the Bar as well. There were plenty of students studying around me, but there was no one willing to study with me. My study partners who got through law school with me decided to either study away from the crowded dorms or had their own methods that didn't correlate with the traditional schedule of studying. So there I stayed.

It was brutal being away from the people I loved. I was secluded in a room, the walls covered with laws and study materials that I'd posted. Struggling to retain information, I was totally discouraged by the lack of people around me. No one was there to offer hope or understanding.

There had been many times in my life where I'd felt overwhelmed and unsure, but this was definitely Top Five. I was a strong individual overall, but weak in my own ability to stay encouraged when no one else was around. Summer 2012 was one of my defining moments of learning to ride solo. Once that ride was over, I vowed to never ride solo again.

But life had other plans to teach me how to stand during moments of solitude. Once the burden of law school lifted, I relished in reconnecting with family and friends. The amount of relief I gained from no longer having to be socially deprived put me right back in the saddle. Liberated and bold once more, I was able to step forward on my entrepreneurial journey.

Although the journey hasn't been clearly paved, with specific directions to the end goal, I'm confident of my life's purpose. My passion for speaking shifted from advocating in a courtroom to advocating onstage as a motivational speaker. It was made apparent early on that my speaking skills brought support and excitement to those around me.

Alone Again

Just when you think you're out of the woods with one rough patch, you might have to endure another. When it came to starting Made 2 Soar, I realized I had very few people to aide in the process. I am grateful to those who rendered assistance throughout my journey. Many of my supporters, however, were present during show time but absent during the planning stages and behind the scenes.

I had grown so accustomed to having constant support and companionship that it was a little odd when people started disappearing and were no longer there with me. The very moment I expected an overflow of individuals by my side, running with me toward success, there was no one. In my case, there were many reasons for this. From lack of consistency and reliability, to my mistake of trying to fit people in supportive roles that didn't line up with their personal talents. Regardless of the reasons, here are a few lessons I learned in the process:

On the road to success, there will be times you'll have an army of cheerleaders and helpers, and there will be times you'll have to travel alone.

Even if you have a team supporting you today, first realize that tomorrow that support could be gone. For whatever reason, legitimate or otherwise. Those individuals you figured would stick with you for the long-haul could just up and leave. Secondly, even with a team, achieving success will require a certain level of self-sufficiency. Be prepared. Know that your time of standing alone will come. The question becomes this: *How will you push toward your dreams even when you have to ride solo?*

The Gift of Solitude

The gift of solitude seems like an oxymoron. Well, it did to me. But believe it or not, even when being alone feels unmotivating and frustrating, there is so much to gain during these periods. Many times, the reason we enjoy the company of others working beside us is that we secretly covet the approval of others. When you have a team to depend on, over time you begin to rely more on their efforts and less on your own.

Back when I was a student, many of us enjoyed working on projects and homework assignments in teams rather than individually. Aside from the collaboration of creativity, fresh perspectives and socializing, teamwork meant that the assignments were split up amongst the teammates. As a result, we each endured a lesser load. That's all we really ever wanted—to get the work done in the easiest, fastest way possible. What separated the freeloaders from the workers was when we were called upon to perform individually.

At test time, you couldn't rely on anyone else's knowledge. Your performance was strictly dependent upon you. In the same fashion, it's easy to feel unsettled when you're working toward your dream by yourself. There is a time for everything.

On this journey, you must learn to push forward, oftentimes leaning on your own discretion, without the help or opinion of anyone else.

Don't shy away from or despise these times. Understand that you are being made ready to soar. Instead of complaining or worrying about your supporters, support your own dream. Strengthen your knowledge and learn what it will take to get to where you want to be. Take this time to deeply study your purpose and map out your vision. This will prepare you when your time of solitude concludes and people come into your life willing and able to support you.

Without knowing yourself and being confident in your decisions, you will be easily swayed by the opinions and the vision others have for you.

LESSON SEVEN

Giving is A Gift

MADE 2 SOAR

" SUCCESS CANNOT BE
ACHIEVED WITHOUT THE
ACT OF GIVING. "

@madetwosoar

As you come to the final chapter of this book, I should let you know that I end with advice that strikes a personal chord with me. Learning and teaching the principles of success can sometimes be clouded by subjectivity and conservatism. Let me tell you, principles are not effective if they don't attract and penetrate your heart. So whether you're a mover and shaker in the business world, a stern attorney, or a vigorous athlete, I hope my final suggestion causes you to let down your guard and be compelled to implement it in your life.

**As you progress toward success,
recognize and seize opportunities to give.**

Giving and Receiving

The range of looks and perspectives I get from people is mind-boggling. On one end, I have the odd balls (excluding children) who look at me strangely, wondering what happened. Perhaps "odd ball" is a harsh term, but when you're over the age of thirty-five, staring is a bit rude. Then there's the other group of individuals who marvel at me and what I've accomplished. To them, I simply I shrug my shoulders. *At least their reactions are ones of delighted amazement.* Their intrigue also means I hear the following phrases often: "Is there anything you don't do?" and "You inspire me greatly."

Despite their flattering nature, these types of comments make me feel a bit weird because they negate how normal I actually am. I'm just like everyone else. I want to be successful and achieve great things. I'm happy to say that most of the time, unsolicited feedback rolls off the back wheels of my motorized wheelchair. I have learned to assimilate the opinions in such a way that people often wonder if I've ever had bad days.

As a thought-leader and advocate, caring about the thoughts of others is the foundation of my work. Yet the reality is that if I were to truly address the concerns and comments of everyone around me on a daily basis, I would go insane. As I heard another disabled person joke, all the stares and random questions make you feel like a celebrity, except you're not getting paid to put up with the shenanigans of the "normal" population.

Still, the extrovert and kind-hearted person strives to put on a smile and address as many people as possible. And for a long time, I resorted to giving sugar-coated answers to all questions, even the ones that merited a more transparent answer. I simply brushed them off, never giving a platform to all the unscripted challenges I've faced.

Yes, people have seen my publicized story. Yes, people have heard of the main obstacles I've endured, but rarely do I paint the entire picture of my life for others. My mom has never been a fan of my superwoman façade. Whenever she'd witness my times of fabrication, she'd give me the side-eye of disappointment to encourage me to respond more honestly.

As an explanation for my behavior, I figured my glossed-over answers would be uplifting, and motivate others to brush off the problems in their lives. Besides, I was hustling to build a reputation as a "normal" person. Speaking the truth was just too hard. Because if I did, I would become vulnerable, and you'd see me at some of my most embarrassing and lowest moments. While I was busy building my image, however, the reality was that many times, the questions being asked deserved the truth. The askers deserved to know how I overcame moments when depression fought like a deadly assassin to consume my thinking and my worth.

But today, right here, is where I reveal my truth. Here is where I reveal the hardship of having to confront the harsh reality of my life situation. I thank God for the courage to push on and trust Him. It is only because of Him that my darkest moments occurred on rare occasions, and are now a distant memory. But the truth of the matter is that when these moments occurred, they left me feeling overwhelmed with guilt and shame.

Being such a worry wort, my mind wondered and worried all the time. While we all are complicated individuals, I had convinced myself that I was extra-complicated. To be a person whose mind and personality ran on a different track than my physical capabilities meant that every day was a struggle. A struggle between what I wanted to do, and what I was capable of doing at the time I wanted to do it.

A great example is my childhood dream of making a lemonade stand to sell cold glasses in the summer. Spontaneity and creativity would cause me to jump up one summer morning with the idea and a plan to make it happen. But my vision required others to handle the physical tasks of bringing it to fruition. Without the ability to get my closest allies in on the vision, the lemonade stand wouldn't happen. And it didn't. I needed help making posters, constructing a booth, gathering glasses, lemonade, and a cash register. With busy working parents and sisters who weren't confident at selling, making a stand on a Saturday morning wasn't feasible.

To keep myself from disappointment, I began tackling other projects that I knew I could do on my own, on the off chance I had to stand alone on my idea. I called it having a backup plan. Thinking this way has fostered great determination and a zealous outlook on life.

Instead of building a lemonade stand, I began drawing comic books, and found a partner in my fourth grade class to help me sell them. Fifty cents each is what we were charging—until our operation was shut down by our teacher. Apparently it was against school policy to sell anything to students on campus. But even though I found ways to bring ideas to fruition, there were still times I'd look in the mirror and see a person who was close to useless because I had to depend on others for even the most basic tasks. This reality prompted me to wonder why in the world God created me with the personality of an intelligent, strong willed, determined "go getter," and placed me in the body of a person who needs help getting dressed in the morning.

It's a question with an answer I've only recently come to terms with, and which still pushes an emotional nerve in me. Truth be told, even now, in writing the previous few sentences, deleting them and rewriting them, I typed them one last time with a lump in my throat because I remember the hurt associated with my thoughts.

I tried to understand why God would give me so much creativity and so many brilliant ideas, when the execution would most likely require the physical aid of someone else.

It wasn't that I despised my physical looks. Being of short stature, having cute, chubby hands, and short legs with unique feet, was not ugly to me at all. It made me unique. What upset me was the physical hindrances these features came with.

As I moved past my teenage years, I can't tell you how many times I worried that I might become a burden to my family or to those around me. From getting my laptop out and placing on a table for me to write this book, to fetching out-of-reach supplies so I can paint a painting… the list is endless.

While I'm unbelievably grateful for those who assist me, there are times I'm only smiling on the outside. Inside, I'm desperate for independence. You see, when you're given a life like mine, you can feel like you're on the receiving end of help way too many times to be of value to someone else. And no one really understands what you're going through unless they've been in your situation. For that reason, there was a period of my life when I thought I had to fight alone, and find a way to bite the bullet of dependency to stop it from shattering my very existence.

Until Something Happened...

I had a spiritual encounter with my Creator, who made visible just how much I was worth. I wasn't shown how much others have done for me, but the impact I've had on others. This impact is a direct result of the seeds I've sown into the lives of those around me. Seeds of laughter, advice, time, concern, prayers, and thoughts... seeds that I didn't realize I was scattering around to everyone with a fertile ground to accept.

Unselfishly and without notice, I was giving hope away. Even little pieces of myself I didn't think mattered—a laugh, a kind word—ended up producing so much fruit. Glimpsing this helped bring me to the other side of my reality. I am incredibly valuable with so much more to give; I was sure of it. What else? That was up to me to discover and implement. But at that moment I was so transformed, so liberated, that I could *feel* freedom from my burdens. And there's no greater feeling than realizing your outlook has changed and that your situation isn't as bad as you imagined.

I became convinced that I was made to soar in life, not based solely on what I might attain and enjoy, but so I could help others get off the ground.

What do I Have to Give?

What I had to give was a question I pondered for days after my encounter. And honestly, it's a question that has become part of my platform of success. Life is give-and-take. You build give-and-take relationships with people all the time. But do you realize it? When you understand that your very existence is a gift given to you, you have no reason not to reciprocate. Plain and simple, absolutely no one should have a reason to not give back. This is especially true if you're looking for new experiences in life. No one whose hands are tightly gripping what they have is able to receive. I am continually amazed by how many people want success, but carry around excuse after excuse for not giving. People want change in their lives, yet constantly take and hold on to every little thing they have. They feel like they can't afford to give.

I hope that some part of this book has helped you to know that you were made to soar. But being made to soar doesn't imply achieving material wealth only. It means that you already possess what the world needs. What do you have to give? A whole lot. And you may be wondering: *how can that be if I'm reading this and haven't yet reached the level of financial breakthrough I'm striving for?*

Again, we go back to the issue of money. Contributing to great causes isn't just about financial contributions. Some of it is, of course. But your record of giving can start now even if you find yourself without any money at all.

Some of the greatest gifts to give aren't monetary.

Don't be deterred by our society's glorification of celebrities and other wealthy individuals who give to charity as if it's the only means of making a difference.

Having millions of dollars opens the gate wider for you to make an impact, but so does having a great attitude and helpful personality. I cannot stress this enough. Money is not the only way to be a blessing and make your mark on this world. Give of your time, expertise, or even your experiences in life. I guarantee there is a young person who can benefit greatly from your resources and experiences. Even offering a genuine smile and polite "hello" can change the outlook of someone's day. And when I learned that I was capable of giving in this way, I was freed from the embarrassment of having to receive help myself. For I knew there was a greater purpose for my situation.

Being Liberated by Giving

Success cannot be achieved without giving. Altruism build character, elevating your priorities from self-centered to self-sacrificing. Nowadays we shudder at the thought of lending ourselves for the betterment of others. Oftentimes this is because we've suffered from giving in the wrong place, at the wrong time, to the wrong person. It's tough to even think about giving when you've been taken advantage of, abandoned, or even tricked into giving, and you end up suffering a loss.

Don't let this surprise you, but there is a right and wrong way to give. If you'd like to give the right way, be sure that your giving is intentional. Don't let it be solely driven by your heart and emotions, but incorporate wisdom and solid thinking. The biggest mistake you can make is to cease giving because of a past error in judgement.

Recognize your mistake, correct your thinking, and move on from the experience. Sure, in the past I've fallen into the trap of giving so much that I neglected my own needs. But today I recognize there's nothing that can stop me from making the difference I know I need to make. When I look at my history, I see many generations of people who worked hard and gave of themselves so that I might enjoy the life I have today.

My ability to reflect isn't limited to my story. However, if you're reading this book, I guarantee there was some person somewhere in your history who sacrificed and set aside their personal gratification with the thought of you being where you are today. You now owe it to the next generation and your neighbor, your brother or sister, to give.

Giving produces greatness.

You know, they don't call it the gift of giving for no reason.

And it's not because you should give based on potential returns. Your return on investment shouldn't be the focal point of rendering a noble act.

Through genuinely giving, you build character and refine your moral compass. By bearing the struggles or challenges of another person, you alleviate their suffering. Acting selflessly adds value to your own life and makes you a better person. And the better a person you become—whether financially, spiritually, or emotionally—the more you can pour back into the lives of others.

Giving is a continuous cycle that makes life better for all of us. If you don't become familiar with doing acts of kindness, then sadly, you'll never understand the true essence of what it means and feels like to be successful.

When you give to others, you are simultaneously investing in yourself.

LET'S SOAR!

Think about yourself, your family, friends, and community. In what ways can you give to each of these entities, starting with yourself?

Give to YOU:

_____

_____

_____

_____

_____

Give to OTHERS:

_____

_____

_____

_____

_____

MY CONCLUSION

We Are Made 2 Soar!

It is 4:45 am one Monday morning, and the cool of the night hasn't made way for the sun to rise. My sister, Melissa, loads the final duffel bag that I transported on the back of my wheelchair into my blue Chrysler Town and Country. We both take a mental pause to be sure we aren't leaving anything behind. Then she pulls out my metal ramp to load me and jumps in the driver's seat. As she puts the key in the ignition and turns it, I whisper a quick prayer under my breath, "Please God, let it start."

Before I can finish my short plea, the van starts up with little hesitation. It's about a fifteen-minute drive to the airport, where we're headed. A short ride away, but a long and nervous one when there's a bent valve in your engine. The van shook the whole way there, but upon being greeted by the runways and the sight of airplanes landing, my nervousness decreased. I figured we could walk the rest of the way if the van failed us. But thankfully, we arrived. Unloaded. Checked the car.

Our first task after entering the airport lobby is to check my wheelchair for boarding. Planning and taking trips is fun but can be a hassle. There's a lot of extra preparation one must take when traveling with a wheelchair, especially an expensive one with odd measurements and heavy-duty, monstrous batteries. To my delight, the Delta agents greet me with smiles. They remember me from my visit a few months ago. I had assumed traveling would pose a challenge, and had taken the initiative to pay them a visit two months before to confirm my ability to fly.

With identification cards in hand, we approach an agent. She checks our bags and my wheelchair ramp as luggage, then turns her attention to my chair.

"So, you're traveling with your wheelchair, correct?"

I nod with a smile. She goes on.

"Now, is your battery a wet cell or a dry cell battery, ma'am?"

asks the agent, looking at me through glasses perched low on her nose.

I'm immediately apprehensive—I'd called a month ago to confirm with my wheelchair distributor that I had gel cell batteries.

"Ummm, wet or dry? I know I have gel cell batteries," I said hesitantly.

After looking at her computer screen as to see if gel cell batteries are an option for her to click, she looks back at me. With slight concern, she says, "Let me go get the other agent, Rick. Hang tight."

In spite of all my precautionary measures, I should've known a curveball would still be thrown. Here was the dilemma: Custom wheelchairs are like people; they are unique, and their size is unique to each chair owner. Now although I'm just "a little thing," my wheelchair has a big caboose in the back to house the elevation features of my seat. Additionally, most motorized wheelchairs are powered by a wet cell, dry cell, or gel cell battery. If the contents of a battery are fluid enough, they can flow out of their compartment and subsequently be hazardous and destructive to the plane. During my research, I was informed that gel cell batteries would not spill and thus didn't need to be stored in a special container.

When Rick shows up, he takes a quick look at my chair and says, "I know you said you have gel cell but looking at it, you likely have wet cell batteries to power your chair… and I don't know. I have to check with the maintenance guys to see if we even have those special containers to put your batteries in."

This is not what I want to hear with only fifty minutes left before my flight. While I'm pretty certain about my batteries being okay to travel without any extra measures being taken, I sure don't want to risk my life from an error on my part. I take a deep breath and exhale slowly, telling myself, *It's cool. They just need to get the containers, that's all.*

Lo and behold, they don't have the containers in stock.

Panic mode activates. We go through security and sit in the waiting area to wait for Rick to come up with a solution. In the meantime, I call my wheelchair manufacturer. After twenty minutes on hold, I finally get ahold of someone familiar with my wheelchair make and model. I somehow find a way to calmly explain my concern and the importance of determining the travel specifications for my batteries.

"Your Permobil chair is operated on gel cell batteries. Gel cell batteries do not spill their contents and can remain in the back of your chair without a special container."

These words from the manufacturer's representative bring an immense amount of relief. I immediately scan the airport terminal for Rick. Finally, my eyes catch him walking my way. With my hand over the phone receiver, I whisper, "They are gel cell batteries and do not need to be stored in a container." With a smile, he gives me a thumbs up and relays the information to the baggage handler who arrived to take my chair.

I'm on my way to El Paso, Texas to address hundreds of educators, and nothing is going to stop me.

Thirty minutes pass before the flight attendant requests my attention to check my ticket. When she upgrades me from coach to economy comfort, my feeling that everything will be alright intensifies. We finally board, Melissa carrying a computer bag on one arm and me on the other, and find our seats. I certainly don't need the extra leg room, but I'm happy Melissa can stretch out and enjoy the complimentary snacks.

Being one of the first on the plane, I watch as everyone who walks by glances down to my seat, discovering me there. There are many double takes and obvious stares. At this point, I don't care.

It's not even 8:00 am, and I've already experienced a roller coaster of emotions. But I pull down my lap desk from the seat in front of me, then turn to Melissa to take a quick selfie for social media. We are both cheesing hard, which defeats our attempt to look cool. The plane hasn't moved yet, but we are already on cloud nine.

You see, just a year ago, I'd been chasing after any motivational speaker who could find time in their schedule to mentor me. I attended many meetings and community clubs hoping to establish relationships, and to learn how to break into the group of movers and shakers who were well known in the community. I was armed with a vision plan that I'd written because I could clearly see my future self reaching out and inspiring people I'd never met. Around that time, I also spent a good chunk of my savings establishing Made 2 Soar, designing and purchasing business cards, rack cards, and brochures, all of which I hoped would open the door for me to speak publicly.

Finally, here I am on a plane, travelling to my first out-of-state speaking engagement. It's hard to believe. As our plane begins to roll down the runway, we put on our seatbelts, lie back, and enjoy the rush of acceleration. We lift up so smoothly. I glance out the window to watch as all the buildings, trees, and cars become mere specs beneath us.

I close my eyes to give thanks, and when I open them, I see fluffy clouds and rays of sunshine. Everything is so peaceful, nothing but the sky in sight. My mind and soul are so at ease. Since there are no issues on the plane, I realize that *all of my problems were on the ground.* Those challenges and naysayers, my worries and distractions... all of them are beneath me.

My view shifts as I soar to great heights. When the clouds break, a view of the distant ground challenges me to ask, *What are we doing with our time down on earth? Are we spending time focused on things that don't matter or contribute to our success?*

The longer we fly, the more my purpose in life is validated. I will spend my life encouraging others to experience the beauty of soaring. Even if that means writing a piece of literature, despite the times I've doubted my ability to do so. Even if it means stepping out on faith and sharing parts of my life that were once an embarrassment. Even, if after laboring over this text, I only reach a handful of people. It's all worth it to lift up others and encourage them to spread their wings and fly.

I beseech you to fly boldly and gracefully until every dream, no matter how far-fetched, is realized in your life. Elevating your thinking, standards, and mindset will give you a beautiful view of a life worth living.

You and I, my friends, are Made 2 Soar!

MADE 2 SOAR

INSPIRE YOUR AUDIENCE TO GET OFF THE GROUND AND SOAR!

As a top deliverer of motivational content, Made 2 Soar presents creative and innovative lectures, speeches, artwork and training to students, athletes, corporations and faith-based groups.

We empower other to SOAR beyond their expectations and accomplish greater successes in life.

For more information on how to partner with Monique Johnson and Made 2 Soar, visit us online at www.MADE2SOAR.com

SOAR WITH US ONLINE!

Follow Made 2 Soar on Social Media

www.MADE2SOAR.com